Spatial Data Management

Synthesis Lectures on Data Management

Editor
M. Tamer Özsu, *University of Waterloo*

The series will publish 50- to 125 page publications on topics pertaining to data management. The scope will largely follow the purview of premier information and computer science conferences, such as ACM SIGMOD, VLDB, ICDE, PODS, ICDT, and ACM KDD.

Spatial Data Management

Nikos Mamoulis

ISBN: 978-3-031-00756-9   paperback
ISBN: 978-3-031-01884-8   ebook

DOI 10.1007/978-3-031-01884-8

A Publication in the Springer series
SYNTHESIS LECTURES ON DATA MANAGEMENT

Lecture #21
Series Editor: M. Tamer Özsu, *University of Waterloo*
Series ISSN
Synthesis Lectures on Data Management
Print 2153-5418   Electronic 2153-5426

Spatial Data Management

Nikos Mamoulis
University of Hong Kong

SYNTHESIS LECTURES ON DATA MANAGEMENT #21

ABSTRACT

Spatial database management deals with the storage, indexing, and querying of data with spatial features, such as location and geometric extent. Many applications require the efficient management of spatial data, including Geographic Information Systems, Computer Aided Design, and Location Based Services. The goal of this book is to provide the reader with an overview of spatial data management technology, with an emphasis on indexing and search techniques. It first introduces spatial data models and queries and discusses the main issues of extending a database system to support spatial data. It presents indexing approaches for spatial data, with a focus on the R–tree. Query evaluation and optimization techniques for the most popular spatial query types (selections, nearest neighbor search, and spatial joins) are portrayed for data in Euclidean spaces and spatial networks. The book concludes by demonstrating the ample application of spatial data management technology on a wide range of related application domains: management of spatio-temporal data and high-dimensional feature vectors, multi-criteria ranking, data mining and OLAP, privacy-preserving data publishing, and spatial keyword search.

KEYWORDS

spatial data management, geographical information systems, indexing, query evaluation, query optimization, spatial networks

To Elena, Vasili, and Dimitri
for their love and support

To Dimitri and Thalia
for bringing me up well

Contents

Preface

Spatial database management deals with the storage, indexing, and querying of data with spatial features, such as location and geometric extent. The field emerged from Geographic Information Systems (GIS) and Computer Aided Design (CAD) applications, from which it became apparent that there is a need for the efficient management of large-scale spatial data. More recently, Location Based Services (LBS) brought spatial data management needs to common users, who routinely run spatial queries on their computers or mobile devices.

Although the evolution of spatial data management was mainly driven by the need to provide efficient support for the ever-increasing volume of spatial information, in applications such as GIS or LBS, the resulting indexing and query evaluation techniques find application in non-spatial data management as well. In many applications, data can be modeled as low-dimensional points in a feature space; then, spatial data management can be used to facilitate search or analysis. Areas where spatial data management technology is commonly applied include data mining and warehousing, multimedia information systems, bioinformatics, and scientific data analysis. For example, nearest neighbor retrieval, a classic spatial operator, is directly used in classic data mining tasks such as clustering and classification. In addition, Computational Geometry textbooks expose numerous cases of modeling data as high dimensional objects and using geometric search operations to search them.

Many industrial products include spatial data management elements. Major database systems vendors have extended their products to handle spatial data. Examples include the IBM DB2 Spatial Extender, Oracle Spatial, and Microsoft SQL Server 2008. Open-source database products followed a similar path (e.g., PostGIS in PostgreSQL, MySQL, SpatiaLite in SQLite), showing that the support of location and geometry types is essential in any DBMS. Besides database engines, GIS products traditionally support spatial database management. Examples include the spatial data engine by ESRI, Smallworld VMDS, and the open-source GRASS GIS. Since 1994, the Open Geospatial Consortium (OGC), an international voluntary consensus standards organization, supports the development and implementation of open standards for spatial data modeling and sharing.

Integrating spatial data into a traditional (relational) database system is not trivial. The design of the system has to change at both logical and physical layers. First, new and more complex data types must be introduced to model the geometry of objects. Second, conventions should be followed for the representation of spatial data; for example, should objects be approximated and represented as collection of simple geometric constructs (like points and lines) or should they be considered as sets of fine spatial granules (i.e., pixels)? Depending on the targeted applications, one design choice may be better than the other. Third, new query operators have to be introduced, according to common search tasks on spatial data (e.g., spatial selection, nearest neighbor, spatial join). These operators should carefully be integrated with existing relational algebra operators for non-spatial data types. Query languages and query evaluation techniques must be redesigned accordingly. Finally, new indexes for spatial data types should be integrated into the system and modules such as the query optimizer and the concurrency control manager must be updated.

The objective of this book is to provide background on spatial data management issues and techniques to students, researchers, and practitioners. The focus is not on spatial data modeling or query language support for spatial data. Instead, we describe in detail the technology used by the majority of systems in indexing and querying large collections of spatial data objects. Although most of the book can be read by audience with a general background in computer science, it would be more appropriate for readers to be knowledgeable on introductory concepts on database management, including database design, the relational model, query languages, storage and indexing. Part of this book evolved from lecture notes authored in the summer of 2005 for the graduate course CSIS7101 Advanced Database Technologies, offered at the University of Hong Kong.

The book consists of seven chapters. In the introductory Chapter 1, we give an introduction to spatial data modeling and provide an overview of the applications and the historical evolution of spatial data management. In Chapter 2, we provide a formal overview of the most commonly used spatial data model, introduce typical spatial queries, and discuss spatial data management issues. Chapter 3 overviews the spatial access methods, developed for the efficient indexing of spatial objects, with a focus on the dominant R–tree index. Evaluation techniques for the most common spatial query types are reviewed in Chapter 4. Chapter 5 is an introduction on the management of data located on spatial (road) networks. Finally, in Chapter 6, we overview recent applications of spatial data management and trends, including management of spatio-temporal data, similarity search in high-dimensional spaces, top-k and skyline queries, spatial data mining, and spatial keyword search.

Nikos Mamoulis
November 2011

Acknowledgments

Part of the book's material evolved from lecture notes authored in the summer of 2005 for the graduate course CSIS7101 Advanced Database Technologies, offered at the University of Hong Kong. I would like to thank the students taking the course and my teaching assistants for comments on the course material and the contents of these notes.

Special thanks to Man Lung Yiu and Panagiotis Bouros for reading the final draft of the book and providing constructive comments. I am grateful to M. Tamer Öszu for giving me the opportunity to write this book and for his valuable comments on improving the quality of the content. I would also like to thank Diane D. Cerra for overseeing the progress of the project and C.L. Tondo for his help in the final production.

Nikos Mamoulis
November 2011

CHAPTER 1

Introduction

The volume of spatial data available for processing increases rapidly over the years with the evolution of sensing devices and telecommunication technology. In addition, the digitization of geographic information is providing an opportunity for common users to routinely issue location-based requests. Most data that can be stored and analyzed carry spatial information; as a result, the management of location and geometric features of entities is an essential component of a modern Database Management System (DBMS). The mapping of many data management tasks to spatial management problems and the maturity of the developed indexing and searching approaches for spatial data has rendered spatial data management a core database research area. Spatial Database Management Systems (SDBMSs) manage large collections of spatial objects, which apart from conventional features include spatial characteristics, such as geometric position and extent. The management of such data types is particularly challenging because the mature relational database technology is not readily applicable.

As an example, consider the set of restaurants in a city. A restaurant has spatial and non-spatial attributes. For example, the name of the restaurant or the food type it serves do not carry spatial semantics. On the other hand, the address of the restaurant, although it is non-spatial in its raw form (i.e., an alphanumeric string), is associated with spatial information, i.e., the *location* of the restaurant on the city map. If we store the set in a conventional database, we would be able to answer any query which refers to the non-spatial features of the data objects. For example, we would be able to find the restaurants that serve a particular type of food, or restaurants of large capacity. On the other hand, it would not be possible to run spatial queries on the database. For example, we would not be able to find the *nearest* restaurant to our current location, using relational database operations. An application program that would exhaustively read all restaurant tuples, translate their addresses to coordinates, and iteratively search for the restaurant nearest to a given location would not only be too slow but also tedious to implement. Therefore, the direct support of spatial attributes of entities that are stored in a database and the development of spatial query operators is important. This is the reason why most commercial and research database systems support spatial data nowadays.

A natural question is why such extensions could not be avoided, since there already exist mature Geographic Information Systems (GISs) that support spatial data management. The reason is that the focus of GISs is different compared to that of an SDBMS; the goal of a GIS is to assist the analysis and visualization of geographic data, which is just one class of spatial data. In addition, unlike SDBMSs, typical GISs do not support set operations; further, GIS operations cannot be easily integrated with other database operations (e.g., aggregation or ranking). In other words, a

GIS cannot replace the functionality of a database system, which has a much more general focus. On the other hand, applications with GIS functionality can easily be built on top of an SDBMS.

In the rest of this chapter, we first provide a brief introduction to spatial data types, predicates, and queries. Then, we discuss the necessary extensions that should be performed to a DBMS in order to effectively support spatial data management. Finally, we discuss the historical evolution of SDBMSs and other applications that use spatial data management technology.

1.1   SPATIAL DATA TYPES, PREDICATES, AND QUERIES

The most commonly supported and frequently used spatial data type is location. Location can be expressed with the help of a coordinate system. It can also directly be modeled and stored in a relation schema. In addition to location, spatial objects often have a *geometric extent*. For example, the extent of a restaurant corresponds to its building area on the city map. Storing the exact extent of an object may increase storage complexity and query processing time. Therefore, in most practical applications, the extent is approximated by a simple geometric shape (e.g., a polygon or a polyline). For example, roads are typically represented as sequences of line segments (i.e., a polyline). This representation is often referred to as *vector approximation*, because a vector data structure is used to implement it in a computer. Still, representing and managing object extents adds to the complexity of the database. For example, a polygon may have a variable number of edges; therefore, a fixed-length data type cannot be used for its representation. In addition, evaluating spatial query predicates (e.g., overlap) over complex object extents can be computationally expensive.

Typically, for location-based queries, point representations or coarse approximations of spatial objects are sufficient. Figure 1.1 illustrates the location q of a mobile user, who is interested in the nearest restaurant. Clearly, due to the sparse distribution of the restaurants (i.e., r_1, r_2, r_3) on the map[1], their extent does not affect the query result and they can simply be represented as points. Storing extents and involving them in query evaluation is essential for applications where query results are affected by extents. For example, in GIS applications, storing spatial details of objects is essential (e.g., for map overlay operations which analyze topological relationships between different layers, such as hydrology, roads, etc.)

In most applications, objects are represented by the vector model (i.e., by simple geometric objects, such as points or polygons). In some applications, however, we often have small collections of voluminous objects with great complexity. For example, consider a meteorological map, which defines regions based on recorded temperatures. There are regions with temperature less than 0 °C, regions between 0 °C and 10 °C, etc. These regions are typically too large and complex to be represented by a simple geometric object. In this case, it is more appropriate to use a *field* representation. A typical model, in this class, is the *raster* approximation, where each object is modeled as a *set* of granules (e.g., pixels). Other field representations include triangulation models, the quadtree decomposition, etc. Figure 1.2 illustrates a vector and a field approximation of a geometric object. In this book, we

---

[1]The map is a snapshot of a San Francisco neighborhood from Google Maps. The restaurant locations indicated on the map are imaginary.

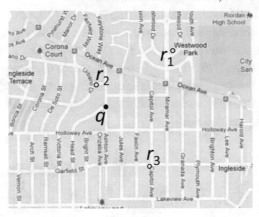

Figure 1.1: Example of a location-based query.

will not consider field representations, which are often used in scientific applications and GIS, but less frequently in SDBMSs.

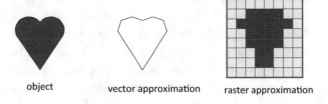

object   vector approximation   raster approximation

Figure 1.2: Vector and raster approximations of a spatial object.

The spatial data types (i.e., location and extent) that can be associated with entities in a spatial database define a new class of *spatial relationships*[2] between such objects. These relationships characterize the relative location and/or geometry between two objects. They can be classified as topological, directional, and distance relationships. Topological relationships (e.g., overlap, inside, contains, disjoint, etc.) model relationships between the geometric extents of objects. In a natural language, for example, when people say "my school is in the park", they imply that the extent of the school is enclosed by the extent of the park. This is an example of a topological relationship. Directional relationships (e.g., north/south, east/west, above/below, left/right, etc.) compare the relative locations of the objects with respect to a coordinate (or cardinal) system. Combined models

---

[2]Spatial relationships are often called spatial relations in the literature. Here, we use relationships, in order to distinguish them from database spatial relations (i.e., tables where at least one attribute is of spatial type). Spatial relationships are not to be confused with relationships between entity sets in the Entity-Relationship model; the latter model general associations that may exist between entities.

for topological and directional relationships exist. Figure 1.3 illustrates some examples. Finally, distance relationships capture distance information between two objects. Distance is the hardest to be abstracted. For example, the interpretation of the claim "I am near the train station", in terms of actual distance to the train station, may be hard even for people who know the claimant. As a result, systems use a reference scale to model distance instead of abstract relationships. Even for topological and cardinal relationships, there are no universally standard models, and the convention may differ from implementation to implementation.

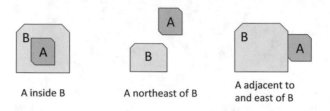

Figure 1.3: Examples of topological and directional relationships.

So, what is the role of spatial relationships in a database system? Like ordinal relationships between numerical data types (e.g., equals, smaller than) that are used in predicates of conventional queries (e.g., find all accounts of balance higher than 1M), spatial relationships are used in predicates of *spatial queries*. For example, the spatial selection query "find all road segments intersecting river Thames" uses the topological relationship "intersects" in its selection condition on a relation that stores the road segments of England. Spatial queries are applied to collections of spatial objects, and use spatial relationships in their predicates. Such predicates are called *spatial* predicates, to differentiate them from conventional query predicates that we find in relational databases. A spatial DBMS supports a set of spatial query operations together with relational operations. The most common spatial query type is the spatial selection, which asks for objects in a relation that satisfy a spatial predicate with a reference object or user-specified region. For example, graphical tools over GISs allow users to define *query windows* and return objects of interest inside these regions. In addition, by typing an address at Google Maps, we implicitly run a spatial selection, which returns points of interest in the vicinity of the location specified by the address.

Additional common spatial query classes are nearest neighbor queries and spatial joins. The former request for the set of closest objects to a reference location. For example, mobile users often use location-based services to browse the closest points of interest to their current location (e.g., nearest gas stations, nearest restaurants, etc.). Figure 1.4(a) illustrates the results of a "nearby pizza restaurants" query from a location at the center of Amsterdam, returned by Google Maps. The spatial joins take as input two collections of objects (e.g., roads and rivers) and a spatial relationship (e.g., intersects) and finds the pairs of objects from the two sets that satisfy the predicate (e.g., pairs of road segments and river segments that cross each other). Figure 1.4(b) shows results of a spatial join that finds intersections between streets and canals in Amsterdam. Additionally, more complex queries can be defined by injecting ranking and aggregation elements to the basic spatial query types. Query "find the total number of buildings in Central district" is an example of a spatial aggregation query, which extends spatial selection. Query "rank all pairs of hotels and restaurants in the city, in increasing order of their distance, and return the first 50 pairs" extends the spatial join operation, using the distance spatial relationship, with ranking and limiting. Finally, spatial queries often have non-spatial components in them. For example, the "nearest pizza restaurants" query, illustrated in Figure 1.4(a), in fact applies a non-spatial selection (i.e., food type = pizza) before ranking the restaurants with respect to their distance to the query location.

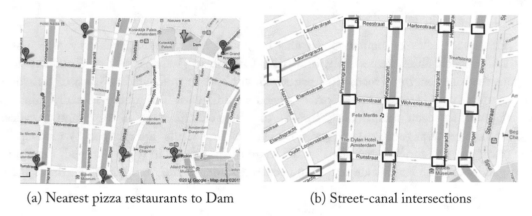

(a) Nearest pizza restaurants to Dam   (b) Street-canal intersections

Figure 1.4: Examples of spatial queries in the city of Amsterdam (maps captured from Google Maps).

1.2   EXTENDING A DBMS TO AN SDBMS

As already discussed, relational database technology is inadequate for managing spatial data. Most database vendors have already responded to the call of extending their systems to include spatial data modeling, language extensions for spatial queries, spatial indexing, and spatial query evaluation techniques.

DBMS technology nowadays supports custom *abstract data types* (ATDs). This extension can readily be used for the definition of the necessary spatial data types. The Open Geospatial Consortium (OGC), an international voluntary consensus standards organization, supports the development and implementation of open standards for spatial data modeling and sharing. The consortium has proposed a specification for spatial ADTs.

The next step is to extend the query language (i.e., SQL) to support spatial queries, based on the defined ADTs. An example of an SQL expression in PostGIS (an open source software program that adds spatial management support to the PostgreSQL object-relational DBMS) is given below.[3]

---

[3]The example is taken from the PostGIS documentation at http://www.postgis.org/documentation/manual-svn/

```
SELECT
  m.name,
  sum(ST_Length(r.the_geom))/1000 as roads_km
FROM
  bc_roads AS r,
  bc_municipality AS m
WHERE
  ST_Contains(m.the_geom,r.the_geom)
GROUP BY m.name
ORDER BY roads_km;
```

This query takes as input two relations `bc_roads` and `bc_municipality`, which store roads and municipalities, respectively, of British Columbia. The objective of the query is to compute the total length of roads fully contained within each municipality. Each of `bc_roads` and `bc_municipality` contain a spatial attribute `the_geom`. The query spatially joins the two relations: for each municipality, the set of roads contained in it are found (predicate `ST_Contains(m.the_geom,r.the_geom)`). Then, the join results are grouped by municipality name (`m.name`), and for each municipality the lengths of the roads in it are summed. Finally, the municipalities and the lengths are output in decreasing order of their total road lengths as shown below:

```
name                         | roads_km
-----------------------------+------------------
SURREY                       | 1539.47553551242
VANCOUVER                    | 1450.33093486576
LANGLEY DISTRICT             | 833.793392535662
BURNABY                      | 773.769091404338
PRINCE GEORGE                | 694.37554369147
...
```

As illustrated above, the core SQL language semantics are not changed. The language extension includes the introduction of spatial ADTs and a set of new functions that define predicates based on spatial relationships.

Apart from providing means for modeling spatial data and expressing spatial queries, the spatial DBMS should also care about the efficient evaluation of these queries. Spatial query evaluation in a brute force manner can be highly inefficient for two reasons. First, the geometry of the objects could be too complex; therefore, testing a query predicate against each object in a database would result in a high computational cost. Second, exhaustively testing all objects of the relation against a spatial query predicate requires a significant amount of I/O operations, for large databases.

In a spatial DBMS, the first issue is handled by storing, together with the exact geometry of each object, a cheap *spatial approximation*, which can be used as a fast filter. The most commonly used approximation is the *minimum bounding rectangle* (MBR); the MBR of an object is the minimum rectangle which *encloses* the geometric extent of the object. First, the query predicate is tested against the MBR of the object; if the MBR passes the *filter step*, then the exact geometry of the object is tested against the query predicate (*refinement step*).

The second issue of avoiding checking all objects (even their approximations) can be handled by indexing. Spatial indexing (and spatial query evaluation in general) evolved from data structures that support efficient multi-dimensional range search algorithms in Computational Geometry. The dimensionality and extent of spatial objects does not allow for the definition of an index with theoretical guarantees in its search cost (like the B–tree in relational databases). Still, multi-dimensional indexes that work very well in practice exist, especially for low-dimensional spaces, i.e., the 2D or 3D spatial domain. The most dominant spatial access method is the R–tree. The R–tree defines a hierarchical partitioning of the spatial domain by grouping nearby objects into disk blocks and using as search keys the MBRs of the objects and groups thereof. The hierarchical structure of the index guides search and prunes sub-trees (and the corresponding objects indexed in them) that do not satisfy the query predicate. Other popular indexing methods include grid-based space decomposition and B–tree indexing after transformation to 1D space, using space-filling curves.

The introduction of spatial search operations and spatial indexes into a DBMS increases the evaluation options for complex queries that may involve spatial and non-spatial components. As a result, cost and selectivity estimation models for spatial query components are used in combination with those of relational operations to upgrade the DBMS query optimizer. The query optimizer now has to select among a richer set of potential evaluation plans for a given query.

1.3   HISTORICAL EVOLUTION OF RESEARCH AND SYSTEMS DEVELOPMENT

As in most technology fields, in spatial data management, research precedes development. In the 1980's, spatial data management started as an extension to the existing relational database technology to support the more complex data types found in geographical information systems. In this first decade, the research focus was on appropriate index methods for spatial data, given the inadequacy of relational indexes, like the B–tree. This led to the development of a wide range of indexes. In the 1990's, with the emergence of the object-oriented (OO) model, the focus shifted on spatial database modeling by either directly using OO or extending the relational model. The latter efforts led to the definition of the object-relational (OR) model, which is now used by most DBMSs. In addition, the community dealt with the efficient processing of spatial queries, like nearest neighbor queries or spatial joins and the first indexes for data on spatial (road) networks were developed. In the 2000's, research was aligned with the recent trends and application demands: spatio-temporal data management, continuous evaluation of spatial queries on streaming data, data management for spatial data warehousing and mining, geographic information retrieval, to name a few.

In the 1970's, a number of GIS-like systems that dealt with automated mapping and facilities management were developed; their goal was to digitize maps of city infrastructure (e.g., pipes or transmission lines). In addition, early GISs were developed for the management of geographic data (e.g., hydrology). All these systems were standalone and stored data directly on file systems. Since 1981, ESRI has led the development of commercial GIS, with the series of ArcInfo (now integrated into the ArcGIS system). ArcInfo, now in its 10th version, is a full-fledged GIS that supports both field and vector spatial data models. Other known GISs include Mapinfo (since 1986), GE Smallworld GIS (since 1990), and the open-source GRASS GIS (since 1997). Major DBMS vendors have extended their products to handle spatial data. Since 1995, Informix (later acquired by IBM) includes spatial data support and an R–tree index implementation. Oracle included basic spatial data capabilities as early as 1984. When Oracle 8 was released in 1997, it included the Oracle Spatial extension, with mature spatial indexing and search support. IBM DB2 includes a Spatial Extender since the late 1990's, which supports spatial data types, spatial predicates, and grid-based spatial indexing. In its 2008 release, Microsoft SQL Server provided spatial data management support, with a choice on indexing (multi-layer grids, space-filling curves and B–trees). The Boeing Company's Spatial Query Server (since 2006) is a commercially available product which enables a Sybase database to contain spatial features. Popular open-source database products, developed in the 2000's, followed a similar path (e.g., PostGIS in PostgreSQL, MySQL, SpatiaLite in SQLite), showing that the support of location and geometry types is an essential element in any DBMS.

1.4   SUMMARY AND OUTLINE

Spatial data management is an essential component of a modern DBMS, due to the fact that many data carry spatial semantics and there are many contemporary applications that search and analyze data spatially. Although Geographic Information Systems are capable of managing large-scale data, they cannot replace an SDBMS, due to their different scope and design.

Spatial objects are characterized by a location and/or a geometric extent. Different approximation levels for the geometry of objects are possible, depending on the demands of the application. The relative location and geometry of objects define spatial relationships between them, which can be used in predicates of spatial queries. The most basic spatial query types are spatial selection, nearest-neighbor search, and spatial joins. Extending a DBMS to support spatial data requires changes at all layers: data modeling, query languages, storage and indexing, query evaluation and optimization, transaction management, etc.

The goal of this book is to provide background on spatial data management issues and techniques to students, researchers, and practitioners. The focus is not on spatial data modeling or query language support for spatial data. Instead, we describe in detail the technology used by the majority of systems in indexing and querying large collections of spatial data objects. Although most of the book can be read by audience with a general background in computer science, it would be more appropriate for readers to be knowledgeable on introductory concepts on database management, including database design, the relational model, query languages, storage and indexing.

Chapter 2 describes the special features of spatial data and explains why relational database systems cannot effectively manage such information. We also overview three classes of spatial relationships that can be used as condition predicates in spatial queries and describe the most common spatial queries that apply on object collections. Chapter 3 provides an introduction on spatial data indexing and briefly outlines the key issues of this problem. After reviewing some early indexing efforts and discussing their drawbacks, we describe in detail the R–tree, a powerful index for spatial data. Issues like dynamic construction and maintenance of R–trees, as well as bulk loading R–trees for a static collection of spatial objects are covered. In Chapter 4, we show how the most common spatial query types can be processed in a Spatial Database System, including spatial selections, nearest neighbor queries, and spatial joins. Chapter 5 is an introduction on the management of data located on spatial (road) networks. We discuss how the replacement of Euclidean distance by the shortest path distance affects indexing and query evaluation. Finally, Chapter 6 overviews recent developments and trends on spatial data management, including management of spatio-temporal data, similarity search in high-dimensional spaces, top-k and skyline queries, spatial data mining, and spatial keyword search.

BIBLIOGRAPHIC NOTES

There are several textbooks devoted to spatial data management. The textbook by Shekhar and Chawla [2003], based on an earlier survey by Shekhar et al. [1999], is a comprehensive coverage of spatial databases technology. An earlier textbook by Rigaux et al. [2001] focuses on GIS applications. In their book on Object-Relational DBMSs, Stonebraker et al. [1998] discuss the limitations of relational DBMSs to handle complex data types such as spatial. Laurini and Thompson [1992] cover spatial data models, while Worboys and Duckham [2004] discuss implementation issues in systems that manage geographic information. The website of the Open Geospatial Consortium (http://www.opengeospatial.org/) includes up-to-date standards on geospatial data modeling and query languages. Zeiler [1999] presents the concepts and techniques used by the ArcInfo GIS for the design and implementation of geographic databases. Besides, Güting [1994] offers an excellent introduction to spatial databases.

Besides the commercial and open-source systems, which we reviewed in Section 1.3, that support spatial data management, there are also several research prototypes, like Paradise [Team, 1995] and SECONDO [Güting et al., 2005].

Conference series dedicated to research on spatial data management include the annual ACM SIGSPATIAL International Conferences on Advances in Geographic Information Systems (ACM GIS), the biannual Symposia on Spatial and Temporal Databases (SSTD), and the annual IEEE International Conferences on Mobile Data Management (MDM). GeoInformatica is a journal, published by Springer, which covers spatial modeling and databases.

CHAPTER 2

Spatial Data

An object is characterized as *spatial* if it has at least one attribute that captures its location in a 2D or 3D space. Moreover a spatial object is likely to have geometric *extent* in space. For example, we can say that a building is a spatial object, since it has a location and a geometric extent in a 2D or 3D map. As another example, in a large-scale map, we can consider cities as spatial objects with location, but no extent (i.e., we can model them as points).

A collection of spatial objects which have the same semantics is a *spatial relation*. More formally, a spatial relation is a table, where each row corresponds to a spatial object and each column to an attribute of spatial or non-spatial type. Figure 2.1 shows an example of a spatial objects collection and the corresponding spatial relation. In this example, the spatial attribute of each object is modeled by a polyline. Note that spatial objects may have non-spatial attributes (e.g., name). In this example, we have modeled the spatial attribute of an object as a *vector* of spatial co-ordinates. The approximation of the spatial features of an object using vectors is very popular since it is cheap and can be used at multiple resolutions of the data space.

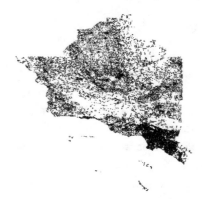

ID	Name	Type	Polyline
1	Boulevard	avenue	(10023,1094), (9034,1567), (9020,1610)
2	Leeds	highway	(4240,5910), (4129,6012), (3813,6129), (3602,6129)
...	...	...	...

(a) a collection of road segments   (b) a spatial relation

Figure 2.1: Example of a spatial relation.

The need for efficient management of spatial objects emerged from Geographic Information Systems (GISs), which provide mechanisms for the visualization and analysis of geographic data. Digitization of geographic information brought to availability large spatial maps of various thematic contents which need to be efficiently analyzed. Spatial databases not only store geographic content. Spatial objects are found in segmented medical images (i.e., objects in an X-ray), components in computer-aided design (CAD), constructs or VLSI circuits, stars on the sky, components of molecular structures, objects in microscopic images, etc.

More and more users are interested in retrieving information related to the locations and geometric properties of spatial objects. Users of mobile devices may want to find the nearest hotel to their location. Astrologers may want to study the spatial relationships among objects of the universe. Army commanders may want to schedule the movements of their troops according to the geography of the field. Scientists may want to study the effects of object positions and relationships in a 2D/3D space to some scientific or social fact (e.g., spatial analysis of protein structures, relationship between the residence of subjects and their psychic behavior, etc.).

The rest of this chapter reviews the types of spatial relationships between objects, summarizes the most important types of spatial queries, and introduces the special characteristics of spatial data that complicate their efficient management.

2.1   SPATIAL RELATIONSHIPS

A *spatial relationship* associates two spatial objects according to their relative location and extent in space. People frequently use spatial relationships in their natural language. Consider, for instance, the expression "my house is close to Central Park." In this expression, *close to* is a spatial relationship which implies an upper distance bound between the two objects *my house* and *Central Park*. This is an example of a *distance* relationship. Other important classes of spatial relationships are *topological* and *directional* relationships.

2.1.1   TOPOLOGICAL RELATIONSHIPS

An object is characterized by the space it occupies in the universe, which can be considered as a subset of the set of pixels in the universe. Conceptually an object has a *boundary*, which is defined by the pixels that are adjacent to at least one pixel outside the object, and an *interior*, which is the set of pixels occupied by the object, but are not part of its boundary. Topological relationships associate two objects based on the set-relationships that hold between their boundaries and interiors. Figure 2.2 illustrates a hierarchy of simple topological relationships that may exist between two objects. Observe that the relationship *intersects* implies one of the *equals, inside, contains, adjacent, overlaps*, i.e., it is a generalization of all of these topological relationships. In other words $intersects(o_1,o_2) \Leftrightarrow \neg disjoint(o_1,o_2)$. Table 2.1 shows how these relationships can be defined by logical expressions on the interiors and boundaries of the objects. For example, object o_1 is inside object o_2 (denoted by $inside(o_1,o_2)$) if and only if the interior of o_1 is a subset of the interior of o_2.[1] Specializations of *inside* and *contains* are also possible, if we consider the potential boundary intersection of the associated objects. For example, in the illustration of the *contains* relationship in Figure 2.2 the boundaries of the two objects intersect. This relationship could be differentiated from another *contains* relationship

---

[1]In fact, the definitions of Table 2.1 assume that both objects have interiors. In the general case, where an object can have only boundary (e.g., points, lines), the definitions are slightly altered. We leave this as an exercise to the reader.

where boundaries are disjoint. In addition, more complex topological relationships can be defined if we consider objects with holes and/or non-contiguous areas.

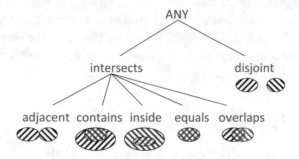

Figure 2.2: A set of simple topological relationships.

Table 2.1: Definitions of topological relationships.	
Topological relationship	**equivalent boundary/interior relationships**
$disjoint(o_1, o_2)$	$(interior(o_1) \cap interior(o_2) = \emptyset) \wedge (boundary(o_1) \cap boundary(o_2) = \emptyset)$
$intersects(o_1, o_2)$	$(interior(o_1) \cap interior(o_2) \neq \emptyset) \vee (boundary(o_1) \cap boundary(o_2) \neq \emptyset)$
$equals(o_1, o_2)$	$(interior(o_1) = interior(o_2)) \wedge (boundary(o_1) = boundary(o_2))$
$inside(o_1, o_2)$	$interior(o_1) \subset interior(o_2)$
$contains(o_1, o_2)$	$interior(o_2) \subset interior(o_1)$
$adjacent(o_1, o_2)$	$(interior(o_1) \cap interior(o_2) = \emptyset) \wedge (boundary(o_1) \cap boundary(o_2) \neq \emptyset)$
$overlaps(o_1, o_2)$	$(interior(o_1) \cap interior(o_2) \neq \emptyset) \wedge (\exists p \in o_1 : p \nsubseteq interior(o_2) \wedge p \nsubseteq boundary(o_2))$
	$\wedge (\exists p \in o_2 : p \nsubseteq interior(o_1) \wedge p \nsubseteq boundary(o_1))$

2.1.2 DIRECTIONAL RELATIONSHIPS

Directional (or cardinal) relationships associate two objects based on their (relative) orientation with respect to a global reference system. Examples of directional relationships are *north, south, east, west, northeast*, etc. The reference system could also be defined with respect to the orientation of a viewer or a reference object. Examples of such relationships are *left, right, above, below, front, behind*, etc. Directional relationships can be subjective. For example, there may not be a clear border between south-west and west. Therefore, spatial data models often use fuzzy definitions of directions (e.g., 20% north, 80% east).

2.1.3 DISTANCE RELATIONSHIPS

Distance relationships associate two objects based on their distance, which is measured by a (geometric) distance metric, e.g., the Euclidean distance. Actual distance values are not always useful because humans tend to classify them in (subjective or objective) ranges. For example, we can divide the domain of possible distances between objects in a city to distances up to 100 meters, characterized by the relationship *near*, distances from 100 meters to 1km, characterized by the relationship *reachable*, distances from 1km to 10km, characterized by the relationship *far*, and distances larger than 10km, characterized by the relationship *very far*. Therefore, distance relationships can be expressed either explicitly (by the actual geometric distance between the objects) or implicitly (by a distance range).

Topological, distance, and directional relationships can be combined to characterize a pair of spatial objects (e.g., "my house is disjoint with, 100 meters from, northwest of West Bank"). Spatial relationships are used to assist the expression of spatial queries. In the next paragraph we will describe some of the most common spatial query types.

2.2   SPATIAL QUERIES

A spatial query is applied on one (or more) spatial relations and asks for objects (or combinations of objects) that satisfy some spatial relationships with a reference query object (or between them). Spatial queries are the reason for devising specialized management methods for spatial data, in the same way as relational queries determine the way relational data are stored, indexed, and accessed.

The most common spatial query type is the *spatial selection* (or *spatial range query*), which asks for objects in a spatial relation that satisfy a spatial predicate with a well-defined spatial region or object. As an example consider a spatial relation that stores information about cities and the query "find all cities intersected by the Danube river". The response set includes cities whose boundaries or interiors intersect the polyline which represents the Danube river. As another example consider a spatial relation storing cities, as depicted in Figure 2.3a, and the query "find all cities within 100 km distance from the point F". In this case the circle with center F and radius 100 km defines the spatial region of the selection and the response set is $\{c_1, c_2, c_4\}$. The simplest selection query is the point query, i.e., we want to find the objects that contain a given point.

(a) a spatial selection on Cities   (b) spatial join between Cities and Rivers

Figure 2.3: Example of two spatial queries on relations Cities and Rivers.

Another common spatial query type is the *nearest neighbor query*, which, given a well-defined reference object q, asks for the nearest object (or for the k-nearest objects) to q in the spatial relation. The query "find the city which is closest to the point F" is a nearest neighbor query, which, when applied to Figure 2.3a, will retrieve city c_2.

Both selection and nearest-neighbor queries apply to a single relation. The *spatial join* is a query that combines two relations, retrieving the subset of their Cartesian product that qualifies a spatial predicate (i.e., a spatial relationship). Formally, given two spatial relations R and S and a spatial relationship θ, the spatial join $R \bowtie_\theta S$ is defined as $\{(r, s) : r \in R, s \in S, r \; \theta \; s\}$. As an example, consider two relations that store cities and rivers as depicted in Figure 2.3b and the spatial join query "find all pairs of cities and rivers that intersect". The response set of this query is $\{(c_1, r_1), (c_2, r_2), (c_5, r_2)\}$.

Besides the three basic spatial query types that we have discussed, there are also additional, more sophisticated operations on spatial data. For example, so far, we have assumed that the spatial objects are *atomic* entities, i.e., they are not decomposable and they are treated as units in set operations. In GIS applications, however, a spatial object may be decomposable and we could be able to express queries that generate new objects, using partial information from the input data. For example, consider a query, which returns the geometries of rivers that pass through a query region, excluding their parts outside the query region. As another example, consider a definition of the spatial intersection join, which instead of returning pairs of objects that intersect, computes and outputs the common (intersection) regions between these pairs. Objects can also be merged to define new, composite objects (fusion). In addition, spatial aggregation operations can be defined by extending the spatial selection operation (e.g., "what is the number of lakes in a given geographic region?"). Finally, complex queries can be defined by combining the basic spatial query operations, we discussed so far (e.g., "list the 5 nearest service stations to my location; list the restaurants (if any) within 100 meters from each of these stations").

Query languages can easily be extended to support spatial query expressions. For example, selection predicates in the SQL WHERE clause may include functions that compare the geometric extents of objects or measure distance between them. In general, the language extensions are straightforward (Chapter 1 contains an example in PostGIS) and covering them in detail is beyond the scope of this book. On the other hand, as we discuss in the next section, efficient spatial query evaluation is non-trivial, due to the special nature of the data.

2.3   ISSUES IN SPATIAL QUERY PROCESSING

The spatial features of an object are typically stored physically as a sequence of point coordinates that define a polygonal or polyline approximation of the object. In the simplest case, where objects are points, a single d-tuple per object is stored (d is the dimensionality of space). While objects can be represented in a straightforward way, access methods and query processing techniques for relational databases are not readily applicable for spatial databases due to the following properties of spatial data:

- There is no total ordering in the multidimensional space that preserves spatial proximity. As a result, objects in space cannot be physically clustered to disk pages in a way that provides theoretically optimal performance bounds to spatial queries.

- The spatial extents of objects add to the complexity of physical clustering imposed by dimensionality and do not allow for a standard and closed definition of spatial operators and algebra.

To comprehend the first issue, assume that we try to sort a set of two-dimensional points using some one-dimensional sorting key. No matter which key we use, we cannot guarantee (for arbitrary point sets) that any pair of objects, which are close in space, will also be close in the total order. This can be demonstrated in Figure 2.4 which shows three orderings of pixels (i.e., cells) on a 4×4, two-dimensional map. These orderings are also called *space filling curves*. No matter which curve is chosen at sorting, we can find a pair of objects for which the distance in the ordering does not reflect the actual distance in space. For instance, points at positions 3 and 12, in Figure 2.4b, are relatively close to each other, but they are very far in the linear order defined by the curve. Thus, there is a lack of a linear ordering method in the 2D (and, in general, multi-dimensional) space that preserves spatial locality for arbitrary data distributions. The implication of this is that we cannot achieve good theoretical bounds for the cost of spatial selections (and spatial queries in general) and that we cannot guarantee that this cost linearly depends on the selectivity of the queries. On the other hand, instances of relational data types (i.e., numbers, strings, etc.) can be totally ordered and the worst-case cost of range queries on them is logarithmic to the relation size and linear to the query output size. Although there exist main memory data structures that provide good theoretical bounds on 2-dimensional range queries on points (e.g., the *range tree*), to date, no dynamic, disk-based access method can provide acceptable worst-case bounds for spatial data.

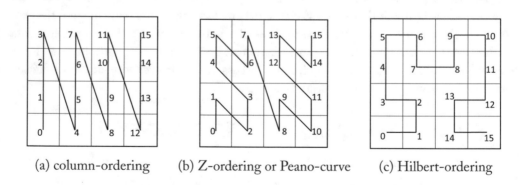

(a) column-ordering   (b) Z-ordering or Peano-curve   (c) Hilbert-ordering

Figure 2.4: Spatial filling curves.

The spatial extent further complicates indexing, since it cannot be modeled by a simple key, even in the 1D space. Consider for instance the problem of indexing 1-dimensional intervals. Sorting the intervals according to one end-point or some other uniquely defined point (e.g., the interval's center) does not optimally solve the problem of finding intervals that intersect a point. Some main memory solutions (e.g., interval tree, segment tree) cannot be straightforwardly transformed to disk-based indexing methods. More importantly, they cannot be applied to objects of higher dimensionality and more complex extent.

Apart from the indexing problem, the complex geometry of the objects renders the evaluation of spatial predicates inefficient when applied directly on their exact representations. Consider, for instance the set of objects depicted in Figure 2.5a and a query that asks for all objects that intersect the window W. The cost of applying the query directly on the polygonal representations is high, since expensive computational geometry algorithms are required. More specifically, the cost of checking the intersection of two polygons is in the worst case $O(n \log n)$, where n is the total number of edges in the polygons. In order to reduce the large computational overhead of spatial queries, along with each object, a *conservative* approximation is stored. The most common approximation is the *minimum bounding rectangle* (MBR), which is the minimum rectangle that encloses the object.

The spatial query is then processed in two steps. During the *filter* step, the query is applied on the object MBRs. If the MBR of the object does not qualify the query, then the exact geometry does not qualify it either. This can be demonstrated in Figure 2.5b, where MBRs that do not intersect W do not enclose objects that qualify the query. The filter step is a computationally cheap way to prune the search space, but it only provides candidate query results. During the *refinement* step, the exact representations of the candidates are tested with the query predicate to retrieve the actual results. In Figure 2.5c, observe that only two from the three candidates are query results. In some cases the refinement step can be avoided. For example, if at least one side of the MBR is inside W, then the object definitely intersects W.

For most (topological) spatial relationships between two objects, the tightest relationship that should hold between their MBRs is *intersects*. As a result, in many cases, when we are talking about spatial queries, we refer to the filter step (which is essential for pruning large parts of the database), considering the intersection spatial relationship.

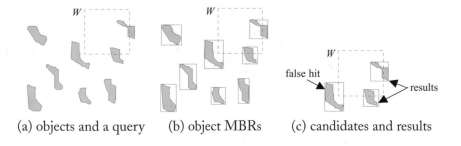

(a) objects and a query   (b) object MBRs   (c) candidates and results

Figure 2.5: Two step query processing using object approximations.

2.3.1   EXTENT OR NOT?

More often than not, in large collections of spatial objects, the extents of the objects are very small compared to the world where they exist. For example, cars and buildings on a city map are very small compared to the area of the city. The impact of this is that for queries that implicitly or explicitly refer to a large area of the map, the object extents play negligible role to the query result; approximating the objects as points and treating them as a point dataset would have small, if any, effect to the result of the query.

As a result, in many spatial database applications, object extents could be ignored whenever the scale of the query is much larger than the scale of the objects. For example, it is typical for location-based queries (e.g., find the nearest restaurant) to consider the locations of query and the data objects as points. The technical implication of this is that storage, indexing, and search can be greatly simplified in the SDBMS; the expensive refinement step is not necessary for most queries as details about the geometry of objects are disregarded.

2.4 SUMMARY

Spatial data objects are characterized by location and extent. These features define special sets of relationships between them: topological, directional, and distance relationships. Based on these relationships, we can define new predicates in database queries; spatial queries extend the traditional selection, ranking, and join operations to include spatial relationships. The management of spatial data is challenging because their dimensionality and extent complicates indexing and query evaluation. A common technique to alleviate the high cost of spatial query evaluation is to define cheap approximations of the objects and use them as fast filters. The next two chapters elaborate more of spatial indexing and query evaluation.

BIBLIOGRAPHIC NOTES

Our definition for spatial relations is based on the object-relational data model for complex data management [Stonebraker et al., 1998]. Spatial data modeling in a DBMS has been an important issue, since the late 80's [Laurini and Thompson, 1992], with the development of several, mainly object-oriented, models [Borges et al., 2001, de Oliveira et al., 1997] and extending the UML and ER models [Shekhar et al., 1997].

There has been a significant amount of research on the definition and reasoning with topological [Egenhofer, 1991, Egenhofer et al., 1994, Renz and Nebel, 1999], distance [Zimmermann, 1993], and directional [Chen et al., 2010, Freksa, 1992, Ligozat, 1998, Skiadopoulos et al., 2004, 2007] spatial relationships. Papadias et al. [1995] study the conversion of topological relationships between objects to relationships between their corresponding MBRs. They also show how to apply search for such relationships on hierarchical spatial access methods (e.g., R–tree variants) and compare the effectiveness of such methods.

Güting [1994] summarizes the fundamental and advanced [Scholl and Voisard, 1989] spatial operations, typically implemented in database systems that support geographic data. A nice introduction about the special issues in spatial query processing is given by Gaede and Günther [1998].

The filter-and-refine framework has been considered by early efforts to use DBMS technology for the management of spatial data [Frank, 1981, Orenstein and Manola, 1988].

CHAPTER 3

Indexing

The special nature of multidimensional data stimulated the database community to work on the challenging problem of spatial indexing. As a result, a number of *Spatial Access Methods* (SAMs) have been proposed. The role of a SAM is to group the objects into disk pages such that objects in the same page are close to each other in space. The disk pages are then organized into an index; single-level and hierarchical indices have been proposed. This chapter reviews some of the most important efforts on indexing spatial data, focusing on the R–tree, the predominant spatial access method.

3.1 POINT ACCESS METHODS

Many early SAMs are applicable to low-dimensional points, which are easier to manipulate than objects with extent. Most *Point Access Methods* (PAMs) decompose the space into disjoint regions and group points in these regions together into blocks, which are then indexed with the help of a (hierarchical) directory. The main differences between these methods are on how they define the space partitioning and how they maintain it during data updates. In this section, we describe some of the most characteristic indexes in this class.

3.1.1 THE GRID FILE

A classic point access method is the *grid file*. The grid file divides the space into cells, using axis-parallel hyperplanes. Consecutive cells with a large enough number of points in them are grouped into disk blocks (i.e., the points in each group are physically stored in the same block). A *directory* block holds the mapping between cells and disk blocks for easy access. Figure 3.1 is a simple illustration of the grid file. The space is divided into 16 cells, 9 of which contain points. These points are divided into 3 blocks. The directory (not shown explicitly) maps each cell to a block on the disk (block-ids of cells are illustrated by the different colors). The index can be used to answer a window query (i.e., spatial selection) as follows. First, the cells that intersect the query area are identified. Then, using the directory, the blocks that correspond to these cells are found and fetched from the disk. The points in these blocks are compared against the query range and the results are retrieved. The grid file is constructed dynamically, starting from a single cell (and block) that corresponds to the entire space and splitting using hyperplanes, whenever a cell's capacity exceeds the block size and a single block cannot be used to store it. The grid file has similar properties to hash indexes in relational databases. It is good for static data of relatively uniform distribution, since in that case the points are uniformly partitioned into the cells and the disk space is well utilized. However, for skewed distributions, blocks corresponding to sparse areas may be under-utilized and the directory may become extremely large. In addition, dynamic updates may result in expensive split (or merge) operations, where a large number of cells are affected by a single split.

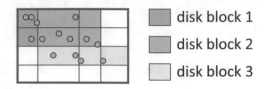

Figure 3.1: A simple grid file.

3.1.2   SPACE FILLING CURVES

Space-filling curves were proposed as early as in 1890, by mathematicians who wanted to create continuous mappings between the one-dimensional and multi-dimensional spaces. This idea turned out to be useful also in spatial indexing. A space-filling curve defines a mapping from a multi-dimensional domain to a one-dimensional domain; that is, every point in space is mapped to a unique number (i.e., distinct points map to different numbers). Therefore, the curve defines a *linear* ordering of the possible points in the multi-dimensional domain. In addition, two points that are close in space are likely to have close mappings, as the curve is a continuous line that fills the entire space.

Figure 3.2 shows the Z-order curve (a.k.a. Peano curve) at three different granularities of the 2D space. The curve is recursively defined as follows. Initially, each dimension is divided into 2^n units ($n = 1$); this division defines four cells, which are ordered by an 'N' curve as shown in the leftmost frame of the figure. At each iteration, the domain of each dimension is doubled; each cell from iteration n is divided into four cells in iteration $n + 1$; the four newly created sub-cells are again ordered by an 'N' curve. The space is divided using as many iterations as necessary, in order to index the multi-dimensional domain at an adequate granularity. In practice, to determine the 1D mapping of a given (x, y) coordinate, the construction of the curve is not necessary. For a given granularity (determined by n), we first construct the n-bit binary representations of x and y. Then, we interleave the bits of x and y, to construct a $2n$-bit number. This number is the Z-order of the point at (x, y). For example, consider the point denoted by the small red circle in the rightmost frame of Figure 3.2. The coordinates of this point are $x = 6$ and $y = 4$, with binary representations $x_2x_1x_0 = 110$ and $y_2y_1y_0 = 100$, respectively. The 6-bit Z-order value of the point is then $x_2y_2x_1y_1x_0y_0 = 111000$, which corresponds to number 56. The Z-order curve is easy to define and nicely preserves spatial locality. Another popular mapping is the Hilbert curve, illustrated in Figure 2.4c.

Using space-filling curves to index spatial data points is relatively simple. A space filling curve is used to define one-dimensional keys for the indexed points. The points are then indexed like relational data with the help of a B^+–tree. The tree can be used to evaluate spatial range queries as

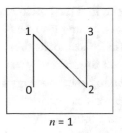 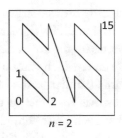 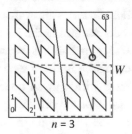

Figure 3.2: Three iterations of the Z-order curve.

follows. Note that the 2D space covered by the query range W contains a set of Z-order addresses. These addresses can be grouped to continuous value intervals on the curve. For example, in the rightmost frame of Figure 3.2, the query range W illustrated by the dashed rectangle contains all Z-order curve values in [8, 15] and [32, 47]. For each interval, we issue a range query to the B^+–tree and retrieve the query results. This way, a spatial range query is transformed to a set of one-dimensional range queries. Because the curve preserves spatial locality, the number of intervals for a random query is expected to be small; therefore, this indexing method is expected to behave well. An additional advantage is that index updates are performed in logarithmic time on the B^+-tree. Space filling curves have been used for indexing spatial data in some systems (e.g., Microsoft SQL Server), and they are mostly appropriate for cases where the spatial data domain and granularity are mostly static.

3.1.3   THE QUADTREE

The quadtree is a tree structure, which is not necessarily balanced, where each non-leaf node has exactly four children. The root node corresponds to the complete 2D space; the children of each non-leaf node divide its area into four equal *quadrants*. Leaf nodes correspond to disk blocks, storing the points that are assigned to the corresponding regions. Space partitioning is done such that each leaf node does not contain more points than the capacity of a disk block. Therefore, the space may be unevenly partitioned by the quadtree; the partitioning follows the data distribution.

Figure 3.3 illustrates a simple quadtree. The left part of the figure shows the distribution of the indexed points and the space partitioning applied by the tree. On the right, the tree structure is shown. The non-leaf nodes are denoted by circles and the leaf nodes by squares. Each leaf node corresponds to a disk page, storing the points that are included in the corresponding partition. In this example, we assume that a disk block can store at most 3 points, so regions with more than 3 points should recursively be repartitioned. The root node has four children corresponding to the top-left, bottom-left, top-right, and bottom-right quadrants of the whole space. Note that the bottom-left and top-right quadrants have at most 3 points, so they do not need to be repartitioned. The points in them are assigned to disk blocks, which are indexed by the quadrants. On the other hand, the top-left and bottom-right quadrants of the root are partitioned recursively.

Spatial range queries are evaluated using the tree structure to find the blocks that overlap with the query area and examining the points in them. The regular partitioning imposed by the quadtree structure allows for smart addressing schemes for the leaf nodes (i.e., disk blocks that contain points). Block addresses can be indexed by a B^+–tree, which can be used to efficiently search for the leaf nodes that overlap with a given query area (similar to the indexing methodology based on space filling curves). One issue with the quadtree is that, due to the regular partitioning it imposes in the whole space and the requirement that each node should have four children, many leaf nodes may be under-utilized (i.e., they may have very few or no children). This issue can be alleviated by techniques that allow multiple leaf nodes to be stored in a single disk block (a method that is also applied for the cells of a grid file).

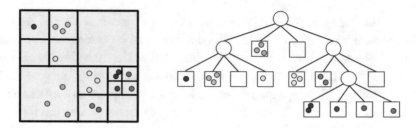

Figure 3.3: Illustration of a quadtree. Left: space partitioning and locations of points. Right: tree structure and distribution of points to leaf nodes.

3.2   INDEXING OBJECTS WITH EXTENT

Point Access Methods (PAMs), some of which we reviewed in Section 3.1, are appropriate for indexing points, not objects with extended geometry. Most PAMs define space decompositions of *disjoint* partitions, which are sufficient for clustering points into disk blocks. However, while a point is guaranteed to be assigned to a unique partition, a spatial object with extended geometry may overlap with more than one partition. For instance, the grid file decomposes the space using an orthogonal grid, each point is assigned to exactly one cell, and adjacent cells are organized to disk pages. The structure cannot directly be used for indexing objects, since grid lines may bisect objects.

One possible way to use PAMs to index spatially extended objects is to apply *object clipping*; an object that is contained in more than one partition is split accordingly and its components are distributed to different disk blocks. For example, consider the set of objects shown in Figure 3.4a. For the sake of indexing, assume that we wish to partition these objects into 3 groups of 4 objects each, such that the minimum rectangular areas that enclose the partitions are pairwise disjoint. Such a task is impossible. Therefore in order to achieve good balance among the partitions, while keeping them pairwise disjoint, the only solution is to clip some objects, as illustrated in Figure 3.4b. This idea can also be applied to indexing based on space-filling curves, where each object is decomposed to a set of granules, each corresponding to a value of the curve, and eventually represented by a set of value intervals on the curve.

Object clipping leads to data redundancy and replication, due to the possible decomposition applied to objects. If the indexed objects have large extents, data replication may affect the performance of indexing. An alternative way to index spatial objects that avoids replication is by considering not necessarily disjoint regions at space decomposition. Figure 3.4c illustrates an example. In order to achieve good balancing in the partitioning, we allow the two rightmost partitions to intersect each other. This results into three partitions, each having four objects. This idea has been employed by the R–tree, which we describe next.

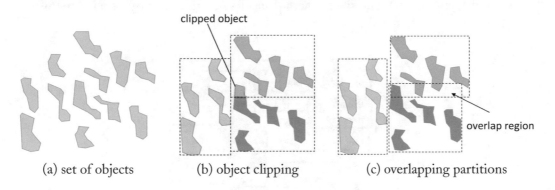

(a) set of objects   (b) object clipping   (c) overlapping partitions

Figure 3.4: Object clipping vs. non-disjoint partitions.

3.3   THE R–TREE

The most popular spatial access method is the R–tree. The R–tree has been implemented in several commercial database products that manage spatial data (e.g., Illustra, Postgress, Oracle, MySQL, Mapinfo). It is a height-balanced tree with structure very similar to the B^+–tree. Like most spatial access methods, the R–tree does not index the exact extent of the objects, but their MBRs. The two-step query processing technique discussed in Chapter 2 is therefore applied; first, the R–tree is used to find fast the object MBRs that qualify the query and then the exact extent of those objects is accessed and verified against the query.

Each R–tree node corresponds to a disk page (i.e., disk block) and consists of entries of the form (MBR, ptr). In leaf node entries, MBR is the minimum bounding rectangle of a data object and ptr is the id of the object. The object-id, equivalent to the record-id in relational database indices, addresses the location of the object in the spatial relation. In non-leaf node entries, MBR is the minimum bounding rectangle of all data objects under the R–tree node pointed by ptr. The number of entries per node is determined by the page size. A constraint of the tree is that each node (except from the root) should be at least 40% full so that disk space is utilized properly. In other words, each node should have between m and M entries, where $m = 0.4M$.

Figure 3.5 shows some object MBRs indexed by an R–tree and a query window W. The query is processed by recursively traversing the nodes (starting from the root) that intersect the window. For example, entry C does not intersect W, thus the subtree pointed by it needs not be examined. The gray R–tree entries in Figure 3.5b intersect W and define the paths that are traversed during search. Notice that although entry **1** intersects W, no object below it is in the response set; intermediate R–tree nodes cannot avoid covering empty space and the overlap between nodes may cause traversing multiple paths even for point queries. However, when a good insertion algorithm that minimizes dead space and overlap between nodes is used, the R–tree performs very well for typical query ranges and data distributions. In this graphical example, the R–tree has a small maximum node capacity M ($M = 4$). In real implementations, the capacity, depending on the disk page size (4Kb-16Kb), can be from a few to several hundreds.

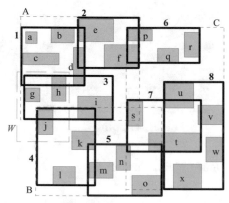

(a) object MBRs (in gray), MBRs of R–tree entries, and a query window W

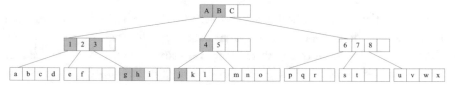

(b) the R–tree; nodes touched by query W are in Gray color

Figure 3.5: A set of MBRs and an R–tree built for it.

3.3.1   OPTIMIZATION OF THE R–TREE STRUCTURE

The R–tree is a dynamic data structure. This means that updates (i.e., insertions and deletions) interleave with search operations. In order to maintain good performance, the tree employs appropriate algorithms that dynamically organize rectangles in the hierarchical disk structure. There are several properties of the tree nodes that affect the search performance of this data structure. We outline them below:

- **The *area* covered by the MBRs of the directory node entries should be minimized**. Observe that the MBR of a directory node entry is defined by the MBRs of all objects in the subtree pointed by it. In Figure 3.5, for instance, the entry labeled **1** points to a disk block that contains objects *a*, *b*, *c* and *d*. The MBR of this entry is the MBR that encloses all these objects. Observe that there is some *dead space* in the MBR of entry **1**. Dead space corresponds to space not occupied by any object MBR under **1**. The (negative) effect of dead space is that the disk block pointed by **1** will be accessed if a query intersects its MBR, even when it does not intersect any object in that disk block. Minimization of the MBRs of all directory node entries implies that the dead space will be minimized and search will be more efficient. For instance, if instead of *a*, *b*, *c* and *d*, we had grouped *a*, *b*, *c* and *x* in the same node, the area of the corresponding node and the dead space would be very large and our tree would not be very effective.

- **The *overlap* between MBRs of the directory entries at the same level should be minimized**. In our running example, consider the root entries *A*, *B*, and *C*. The overlap between these entries should be minimal; otherwise, multiple search paths could be followed by the same query. To see the effect, assume that entry **2** was assigned to node pointed by *B* (instead of *A*). In this case, entry *B* would have large overlap with *A* and *C* and many disk nodes would be visited for a window query enclosing the space around entry **2**.

- **The *margins* of the MBRs of the directory node entries should be minimized**. The margin of a rectangle is the sum of the lengths of its four sides. Assuming a fixed area for a rectangle, its margin is minimized if it is a square. In simple words, the shapes of the MBRs at the directory node entries should be as quadratic as possible, instead of being long stripes. The rationale is that the expected number of fixed-area MBRs touched by an arbitrary query is minimized if they are more square-like. To understand the intuition behind this optimization, consider the problem of Figure 3.6. Here, we have a set of 81 objects to be grouped into 9 disk blocks such that the number of blocks touched by an arbitrary query window (such as the dashed W_1, W_2, and W_3) is minimized. A possible grouping is shown in Figure 3.6b. Another grouping is shown in Figure 3.6c. In this case, the margins of the groups are minimized. Note that the grouping of Figure 3.6c minimizes the average number of blocks accessed by the three queries. Only W_3 is favored by the grouping of Figure 3.6b; thus, this grouping it is not appropriate for arbitrary queries.[1]

- **The average number of entries in an R–tree node should be maximized**. In other words, the tree nodes should be as full as possible. Large occupancy of nodes means fewer nodes (and

---

[1] Observe that the dead space in the grouping of Figure 3.6c is larger compared to the one of Figure 3.6b. This illustrates why grouping of rectangles is a hard optimization problem; optimizing one parameter may negatively affect another optimization criterion. It also shows that margin minimization prevails area minimization. Later, we will see how these metrics can be combined in a good R–tree insertion algorithm.

fewer disk blocks) and shorter search paths from the root to the leaves. On the other hand, packing rectangles to tree nodes allows less freedom for optimal partitioning with respect to area, overlap, and margins minimization.

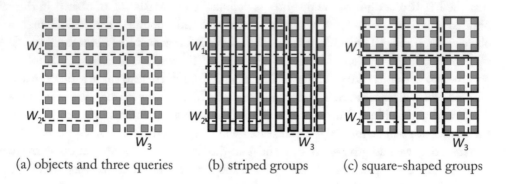

| (a) objects and three queries | (b) striped groups | (c) square-shaped groups |

Figure 3.6: The effect of margins minimization in grouping of MBRs into blocks.

All four optimizations should be considered when updating an R–tree. Assume that we have a (dynamic) set of objects which we want to index. The R–tree can be constructed by iteratively inserting objects into an initially empty tree, consisting of a single (root) block. Once the root becomes full, we need to *split* it into two blocks, considering the optimization criteria. Apart from node splitting, another important optimization is how to choose the most appropriate path when inserting a new object entry in an R–tree.

3.3.2   THE R*–TREE: AN OPTIMIZED VERSION OF THE R–TREE

Several heuristics have been proposed in order to optimize insertion and node splitting in R–trees. Here we will discuss the algorithms employed by the R*–tree, an optimized version of the R–tree. The structure and search algorithms for the R*–tree are identical to those of the R–tree. The only difference between these access methods is the techniques employed for insertion and splitting.

Assume that we have an R–tree structure, where we want to insert a new entry e, containing the MBR of an object and a reference pointer to it. Figure 3.7 describes a recursive procedure that determines the most appropriate leaf node to accommodate e. Function *choose_subtree* takes as input the new entry e and the root node n of the R–tree node and returns the leaf node where e should be inserted. While the current node is not a leaf node, the best entry to be followed is determined based on how its MBR changes after e is accommodated in the subtree under it. For entries pointing to leaf nodes, the minimum increase of overlap is the factor that determines the entry selection. In the case where the overlap increase is the same and minimum for multiple entries, the entry with the least area enlargement is chosen, and if we still have more than one such entries, the entry with the smallest area. For entries pointing to non-leaf nodes, only the area enlargement and the smallest area are considered.

function *choose_subtree*(Node *n*, Entry *e*): Node *leaf*
1.   **if** *n* is a leaf **then**
2.   return *n*;
3.   **if** entries of *n* point to leaf nodes **then**
4.   *fe* := entry in *n*, which will incur the least overlap with
                 other entries in *n* if *e* is accommodated in the node pointed by it.
                 If there are multiple such entries choose the one with
                   the minimum MBR enlargement if *e* is stored under it.
                 Break ties by choosing entry with the minimum area;
5.   **else** //entries of *n* point to directory nodes
6.   *fe* := entry in *n*, with the minimum MBR enlargement if *e* is stored under it.
                 Break ties by choosing entry with the minimum area;
7.   *fn* := *fe.ptr*; //node pointed by *fe*
8.   return *choose_subtree*(*fn*, *e*);

Figure 3.7: The *choose_subtree* algorithm of the R*–tree.

After inserting an entry in an R*–tree leaf node, the node may *overflow*, i.e., it may have more entries than the capacity of a disk block. In this case, the node is split into two new nodes and one entry is added to the parent node of the split one. If the parent node overflows too, it is split recursively.

When splitting a node, we partition a set of rectangles into two groups such that the MBRs of these groups have small areas, overlap, and margins. In addition, each group should contain at least *m* rectangles. A brute-force approach would consider all combinations of possible splits and choose the one with the best quality. However, the cost of such an approach is extremely high. The R*–tree uses the algorithm of Figure 3.8 for node splitting. First, for each dimension *i*, the projections of the rectangles on dimension *i* are considered; these projections are value intervals. The rectangles are sorted into two lists; one using their lower bounds in that dimension and one using their upper bounds. For each list, all possible splits to two groups are considered and the sums of the margins of the MBRs for each group pair are summed. Then the axis with the smallest sum of margins in all distributions is chosen as the split dimension. The intuition is that if we split across the "longest" axis, the resulting nodes will be more quadratic. After the split dimension is chosen, the best distribution along that axis is chosen, this time considering minimum overlap between the resulting groups (and minimum area as a second criterion, in the case of ties).

In order to increase the space utilization of nodes (i.e., to increase the average occupancy of nodes by entries), an additional heuristic is used by the R*–tree. Instead of splitting an overflown node immediately, 30% of its entries (which are far from the center of its MBR) are temporarily removed and re-inserted. The intuition is that these entries may enter some other node and overflow could be avoided. If these entries are re-inserted into the same node, the algorithm proceeds with splitting, since it cannot be avoided. This *forced re-insert* significantly improves the tree structure and makes it less sensitive to the order by which rectangles are inserted. On the other hand, this approach may result in multiple tree paths being traversed during an insertion, which complicates the application of concurrency-control.

function *split*(Node *n*): Node n_1, Node n_2
1.   **for** each dimension *i*
2. $S_i := 0$;
3.   sort the entries using the lower bounds of the rectangles in dimension *i*;
4.   **for** *k*:=*m* to $M + 1 - m$
5.   place first *k* entries in group *A* and the remaining ones in group *B*;
6. $S_i := S_i + \text{margin}(A) + \text{margin}(B)$;
7.   sort the entries using the upper bounds of the rectangles in dimension *i*;
8.   **for** *k*:=*m* to $M + 1 - m$
9.   place first *k* entries in group *A* and the remaining ones in group *B*;
10. $S_i := S_i + \text{margin}(A) + \text{margin}(B)$;
11.   split dimension := dimension *i* with the minimum S_i;
12.   sort the entries using the lower value of the rectangles in split dimension;
13.   **for** *k*:=*m* to $M + 1 - m$
14.   place first *k* entries in group *A* and the remaining ones in group *B*;
15.   sort the entries using the upper value of the rectangles in split dimension;
16.   **for** *k*:=*m* to $M + 1 - m$
17.   place first *k* entries in group *A* and the remaining ones in group *B*;
18.   from all the above groupings (*A*, *B*), choose the one such that
          the overlap between *A* and *B* is minimized;
19.   if there are multiple groupings with minimal overlap,
20.   choose from them the one with the smallest $\text{area}(A) + \text{area}(B)$;
21.   put in n_1 all rectangles from *A*; put in n_2 all rectangles from *B*;
22.   return (n_1, n_2);

Figure 3.8: The *split* algorithm of the R*–tree.

Finally, deletion in an R–tree is handled in a much simpler way compared to the equivalent operation of the B$^+$–tree; if a leaf node underflows after some deletion, all the remaining entries are temporarily deleted and re-inserted into the structure. In this way, the insertion algorithm facilitates optimized re-location of the rectangles and complex processing of deletions is avoided.

3.3.3   BULK-LOADING R–TREES

Given a set of spatial objects, an R–tree can be built for it by iteratively inserting each object into an initially empty tree. However, this method has two disadvantages if all data are available a-priori (static data). First, iteratively invoking the R–tree insertion algorithm is too slow. Second, most of the pages in the resulting tree will have a lot of empty space (typically, the nodes of an R*–tree are 67% full).

A good *bulk-loading* method would build fast, for a static set of objects, an R–tree with maximum node occupancy (and thus minimum height) and high node quality with directory MBRs of minimum area, margin and overlap between them. We can follow the sort-based bulk-loading paradigm, which is successfully used for B$^+$–trees. A brute-force approach would be to choose a sort axis (e.g., the *x*-axis) and sort the object MBRs (or points) with respect to their projection on this axis (e.g., the center of the *x*-projection). The R–tree can then be built in a bottom up fashion by packing M consecutive rectangles (where M is the maximum capacity of an R–tree node), in a leaf node and recursively M consecutive node MBRs at level l to a node at the upper level $l + 1$.

This method constructs an R–tree whose leaf nodes have narrow stripes with large margins as MBRs, which is not expected to perform well for typical spatial queries, as already discussed. A more appropriate sorting key for bulk loading would be the order of the objects in a *space filling curve*. In this way, objects which are close to each other will be packed in the same leaf node with high probability and the areas (and margins) of the resulting nodes will be small. It turns out that using an ordering based on a space filling curve (e.g., the Hilbert curve) tends to create square-like leaf nodes, which however may have a large overlap. Another simple, but very effective method is called *Sort Tile Recursive* (STR).

STR initially sorts the n rectangles with respect to the x-coordinate of their center. After sorting, we know that there will be $L = \lceil n/M \rceil$ leaf nodes in the tree, where M is the maximum capacity of a node. The (sorted) rectangles are then divided into $\lceil \sqrt{L} \rceil$ groups (vertical stripes) and each group is sorted using as a key the y-coordinate of the rectangles' center. The output from this sorting is packed into leaf nodes and the tree is built in a bottom-up fashion. If each of the $\lceil \sqrt{L} \rceil$ groups fits in memory, the secondary sorting of each group does not incur extra I/O accesses and the overall cost of this bulk loading method is minimal.

Figure 3.9 shows for various R–trees the MBRs of their leaf nodes (the MBR collections are truncated on the left for better visibility). The R–trees index a dataset of 191,637 railroad segments in North America. Figure 3.9a shows the resulting nodes if the tree is constructed incrementally using the R*–tree insertion algorithm. Observe that the quality of the partitions is high; however, as discussed, construction is slow and the R*–tree occupies more space on disk compared to packed R–trees. Figure 3.9b shows the resulting narrow stripes if we use sorting only on one axis. Figure 3.9c uses Hilbert curve ordering to sort. Observe that although the resulting leaf nodes have nice shape, at the same time they have large overlap. Finally, the result of STR is shown in Figure 3.9c. The quality of the resulting nodes is quite high, given the fact that they are produced by a bulk-loading method.

3.4 SUMMARY

The first indexing efforts for spatial data resulted in the development of several point access methods, which are appropriate for objects that do not have extended geometry. These approaches can also be used to index extended objects, after clipping the objects, such that they do not overlap more than one of the spatial partitions defined by the access method. Due to the overhead induced by clipping, methods that avoid clipping, but allow overlapping space partitions were introduced. The most important access method for extended objects is the R-tree. There are several efforts on optimizing the R-tree structure and the effectiveness of its update algorithms. The insertion and splitting techniques used by the R*-tree are now considered classic. Bulk loading an R-tree for a static set of objects is also an important problem and several techniques have been developed in the literature.

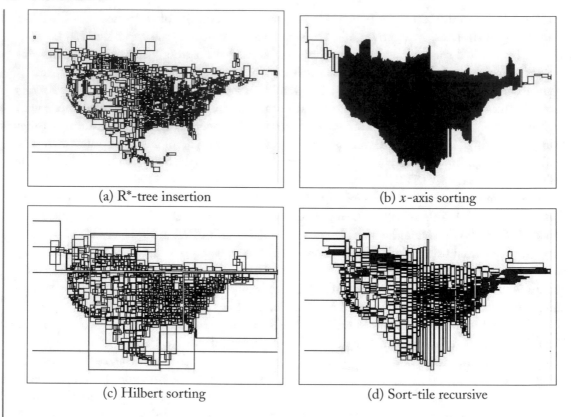

(a) R*-tree insertion

(b) *x*-axis sorting

(c) Hilbert sorting

(d) Sort-tile recursive

Figure 3.9: Leaf node MBRs of R–trees by various construction methods.

BIBLIOGRAPHIC NOTES

Samet's textbooks [Samet, 1990, 2006] provide an excellent technical coverage for the most important spatial data structures for points and extended objects, like space-filling curves, the quadtree, the grid file, the R–tree, etc. Gaede and Günther [1998] wrote a comprehensive survey for multidimensional access methods, which includes the large number of access methods developed in the 80's and 90's and presents a nice classification for them.

Point access methods evolved from data structures developed in Computational Geometry [de Berg et al., 2008, Preparata and Shamos, 1985], to facilitate efficient search in multidimensional spaces. The grid file was one of the first disk-based indexes for spatial data [Nievergelt et al., 1984] and was later extended to a multi-layer grid file Six and Widmayer [1988] to handle objects of varying extent. The use of space filling curves [Sagan, 1994] in spatial indexing and query evaluation was extensively studied by Orenstein [Orenstein, 1986, Orenstein and Manola, 1988] (the Z-order curve, in particular). The quadtree that we describe in the Section 3.1.3 is actually a disk-based variant of the original quadtree proposal [Finkel and Bentley, 1974]. Several variants of this data structure for extended objects have been proposed [Samet, 2006]. Another classic point access method is the k-d-B–tree [Robinson, 1981], which combines properties from the main-memory k-d-tree and the B–tree.

The R–tree was originally proposed by Guttman [1984]. The R^+–tree [Sellis et al., 1987] is a variant of the R–tree, which avoids overlapping between tree nodes at the same level, by applying object clipping. The most popular implementation of the R–tree is the R^*–tree [Beckmann et al., 1990], which we discussed extensively in Section 3.3.2. Recently, a revised version of the R^*–tree has been proposed [Beckmann and Seeger, 2009], which improves the *choose_subtree* function, by disregarding irrelevant entries, allowing the effective (but expensive) overlap minimization criterion to be used also for non-leaf nodes. In addition, an improved split heuristic is used, which achieves node splits of better balancing while at the same time allowing the abandonment of the *forced re-insert* heuristic; this means that a single tree path is now followed during insertion and concurrency-control protocols for trees can readily be applied. An R–tree, which uses a space-filling curve to guide the space partitioning was proposed by Kamel and Faloutsos [1994]. The textbook by Manolopoulos et al. [2005] covers the theory and applications of the popular R–tree index. Techniques for bulk-loading R–trees were proposed by Roussopoulos and Leifker [1985] (sorting based on one dimension only), Kamel and Faloutsos [1993] (sorting by a space-filling curve), and Leutenegger et al. [1997] (sort-tile-recursive packing). The Priority R–tree [Arge et al., 2004] is a worst-case optimal R–tree, generated by an offline (bulk-loading) procedure. A library that enables the use and integration of spatial indexes into applications is offered by Hadjieleftheriou et al. [2005].

CHAPTER 4

Spatial Query Evaluation

The efficient evaluation of spatial queries has been a hot research topic for more than two decades. In this chapter, we review techniques proposed for the most common query types: spatial selections, nearest neighbor queries, and spatial joins. Some of these techniques are now considered classic; they are also applied as modules of more complex queries, or adapted for query evaluation in other application domains (e.g., multimedia and time-series databases, data mining, spatial keyword search).

This chapter provides a comprehensive coverage of evaluation techniques for the most common spatial query types: selection, nearest neighbor search, and spatial join. In the descriptions of the query evaluation methods, the R–tree is considered as the underlying indexing method, whenever a spatial relation is assumed to be indexed. Still, the discussed methods are general enough to be applicable on other spatial indexes, which rely on hierarchical object grouping and space partitioning. In addition, we discuss the issue of spatial query optimization, i.e., how we can extend the database optimizer to consider spatial query operators; for this purpose, models for estimating the selectivity and the cost of spatial query operations have been developed.

4.1 SPATIAL SELECTIONS

A spatial selection asks for the objects in a relation R, which satisfy a spatial predicate with respect to a reference object or region. For example, the query "find all restaurants within 100 meters from my current location" selects, from a restaurants relation, the objects whose spatial extent intersects a disk of radius 100 meters, centered at the querier's location. In GIS applications, spatial selections are commonly expressed by graphical user interfaces where users define selection windows and retrieve objects of interest in them.

The way spatial selections are processed in an SDBMS depends on whether the queried relation R is spatially indexed. If R is not indexed, we scan it linearly and compare each object with the query range. As discussed, database systems commonly employ the two-step processing technique, which tests the object's MBR against the query, before its exact geometry. In the absence of a spatial index, the MBRs of all objects are iteratively tested against the query predicate and the refinement step is only applied to those that pass the filter step. If the relation is indexed (e.g., by an R–tree), then we can use the index to find fast the objects that qualify the filter step. The tree is traversed in a *depth-first* manner, following pointers of entries which intersect the query range. The description of the R–tree, in Chapter 3, already includes an example of how this method works for range intersection queries.

The recursive search algorithm for spatial selection queries is described in Figure 4.1. The algorithm takes three (input) parameters; the query range q, the predicate θ which the retrieved objects should satisfy with q, and an R–tree node n. The results are stored in (output) parameter A. In the first (external) call of the method, n is the root of the R–tree. If n is a leaf node, then for all object MBRs in it that pass the filter step, the exact geometries of the corresponding objects are accessed and the refinement step is applied for them. If n is a non-leaf node, then the MBR of each entry e in n corresponds to the MBR of all objects indexed in the subtree pointed by e. Only if this MBR passes the filter step, there is a chance that we can find an object in the corresponding subtree that qualifies the query. In this case, the method is called recursively for the node pointed by the entry.

For testing MBRs against the query, note that predicate θ' is used instead of θ. θ' is a spatial relationship such that for each object o, (i) $o \, \theta \, q \Rightarrow \text{MBR}(o) \, \theta' \, q$ and (ii) $o \, \theta \, q$ implies that if o is indexed under an R–tree node n then $\text{MBR}(n) \, \theta' \, q$. In other words, θ' specifies a predicate that should be satisfied between the query range and an object's MBR in order for the object to qualify the query. Moreover, θ' should hold between every R–tree node n and q, if a qualifying object o exists in a leaf node that is a descendant of n. For most spatial relationships, the tightest θ' to be used for object and node MBRs during search can easily be derived from the definition of MBRs. For most topological relationships θ' is *intersects*; for example, if object an object a is adjacent to the query range q, then $MBR(a)$ cannot be disjoint with q, but it is not necessarily adjacent to q (it may overlap q). Thus, the search algorithm accesses recursively only those nodes whose MBRs qualify θ' with q; other nodes cannot index objects that may possibly qualify the query.

function $range\_search$(Query q, Predicate θ, Node n, ObjectSet A)
1.   **if** n is a leaf node **then**
2.   **for each** entry $e \in n$
3.   **if** e.MBR θ' q **then** /* e.MBR passes the filter step */
4. o := object with address $e.ptr$;
5.   **if** $o \, \theta \, q$ **then** /* o passes the refinement step */
6.   add o to response set A;
7.   **else** /* n is not a leaf node */
8.   **for each** entry $e \in n$
9.   **if** e.MBR θ' q **then** /* recursive call for the node pointed by e */
10. n' := R–tree node with address $e.ptr$;
11. $range\_search(q, \theta, n', A)$;

Figure 4.1: Processing of spatial selections using an R–tree.

4.2   NEAREST NEIGHBOR QUERIES

The *nearest neighbor* query retrieves, from a spatial relation R, the nearest object to a query object q. For instance, a car driver may ask for the nearest gas station to its present location. Formally, the nearest neighbor of q in R is defined by $\{o \in R : \forall o' \in R, dist(o, q) \le dist(o', q)\}$, where $dist(o, q)$ expresses the (Euclidean) distance between o and q. For objects with extents (and MBRs), we consider the minimum possible distance between the objects. The geometric (i.e., Euclidean) distance $dist(o_i, o_j)$ between two objects o_i and o_j is formally defined by the minimum distance between any two points p_i, p_j, such that $p_i \in o_i$ and $p_j \in o_j$; i.e., $dist(o_1, o_2) = \min_{p_1 \in o_1, p_2 \in o_2}\{dist(p_1, p_2)\}$, where $dist(p_1, p_2)$ is the Euclidean distance between points p_1 and p_2.[1] Note that the nearest neighbor may not be unique; e.g., there could be two (or more) gas stations with the same (minimum) distance from the driver's location. In this general case, we could be interested in *any* nearest neighbor or in *all* nearest neighbors.

The definition can be extended to include a parameter k, that expresses the number of nearest neighbors to be retrieved. A k-nearest neighbor query retrieves the k nearest objects to the query; e.g., the 10 nearest neighbors. The result of the query is a set S of k objects, such that $\forall o \in S, o' \in R - S, dist(o, q) \leq dist(o', q)$.

If the spatial relation is not indexed, then we need to access all objects in it, in order to find the nearest neighbor to a query object q. Observe that the distance between two objects o_i and o_j is lower-bounded by the distance between their MBRs. Formally,

$$dist(o_i, o_j) \geq dist(\text{MBR}(o_i), \text{MBR}(o_j)) \tag{4.1}$$

This is an important property, which we can use to process nearest neighbor queries, using the two-step filter/refinement process. For example, assume that we are in the middle of processing a nearest neighbor query q and after accessing some part of the relation, the nearest neighbor (NN for short) to q found so far is o_{NN}. If for some object o_k, $dist(\text{MBR}(q), \text{MBR}(o_k)) > dist(q, o_{NN})$, we know that $dist(q, o_k) > dist(q, o_{NN})$ from equation 4.1. Thus, we can conclude that o_k cannot be the NN of q, without testing the exact geometry of the objects.

We will now discuss how nearest neighbor queries can be processed efficiently if the relation is indexed by an R–tree. First, however, let us note a property of the R–tree nodes that can help us to accelerate search. Let q be the query object. For any R–tree node n, the following property holds:

$$dist(q, \text{MBR}(n)) \leq dist(q, o_i), \forall o_i \text{ indexed under } n \tag{4.2}$$

Thus, by looking at the MBR of an R–tree node n, we can conclude the minimum possible distance between q and any object which is indexed under n. The intuition is that if this distance is larger than the known distances of objects we have seen so far, we can avoid checking any object that is indexed under this node. Consider, for example, Figure 4.2, which shows a number of objects on the plane indexed by an R–tree (partially shown on the right side of the figure). Let us assume that we already know the distance between q and point p. Observe that the distance between q and node M (i.e., entry M in the root node) is larger than $dist(p, q)$. This implies that *there can be no object o in the subtree rooted at M, such that* $dist(q, o) < dist(q, p)$. Therefore, we can use knowledge about the distance of the objects we have seen so far, to prune large parts of the tree. This *branch-and-bound* heuristic is employed by the nearest neighbor search algorithms, which we are going to discuss next.

[1] In the literature, our definition of $dist(o_1, o_2)$ is often termed $mindist(o_1, o_2)$.

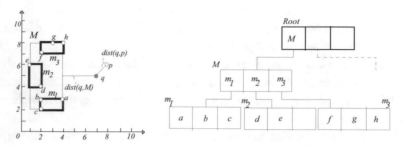

Figure 4.2: Using distance bounds to guide nearest neighbor search.

4.2.1   A DEPTH-FIRST NEAREST NEIGHBOR SEARCH ALGORITHM

The depth-first search algorithm (DF for short) for nearest neighbor queries works similarly to the algorithm used for range search, except that it uses information about the nearest neighbor discovered so far to bound search and prune parts of the R–tree. A pseudo-code for DF is shown in Figure 4.3. Initially, the nearest neighbor o_{NN} is an imaginary object with infinite distance from q and the function is called taking the root of the tree as parameter n. If the currently visited node is a leaf, then its entries (first the MBRs and then the actual objects) are tested to see whether they are closer to q than the current NN of q. If so, the NN information is updated. If the currently visited node is not a leaf of the R–tree, then only those entries whose MBR is closer to q than the current NN may potentially point to a subtree that contains the actual NN.

function DF_NN_search(object q, Node n, object o_{NN})
1.   **if** n is a leaf node **then**
2.   **for each** entry $e \in n$
3.   **if** $dist(q, e.\text{MBR}) < dist(q, o_{NN})$ **then** /* e.MBR is closer to q than its current NN*/
4. $o :=$ object with address $e.ptr$;
5.   **if** $dist(o, q) < dist(q, o_{NN})$ **then** /* found new NN */
6. $o_{NN} := o$;
7.   **else** /* n is not a leaf node */
8.   **for each** entry $e \in n$
9.   **if** $dist(q, e.\text{MBR}) < dist(q, o_{NN})$ **then** /* it is possible that n indexes the NN */
10. $n' :=$ R–tree node with address $e.ptr$;
11. $DF\_NN\_search(q, n', o_{NN})$;

Figure 4.3: Depth-first nearest neighbor search using an R–tree.

As an example, consider a set of objects, an R–tree built for them, and a query point q, as shown in Figure 4.4. Some contents of the R–tree (e.g., the subtree pointed by M_3) are omitted for simplicity. Initially, DF_NN_search (Figure 4.4) is called with the root of the tree as parameter. Since we have not seen any object yet, the NN distance is infinite. Entry M_1 will be the first to be visited. Since the MBR of M_1 is closer to q than the current NN, the algorithm is called recursively for this node and then recursively for its first child m_1, which is a leaf. After all objects in m_1 are examined,

o_{NN} is set to a. When the recursive call for m_1 returns, $dist(q, m_2) \geq dist(q, o_{NN})(= \sqrt{5})$, so we need not visit the node pointed by m_2. The same holds for m_3; thus, the algorithm returns to the call for the root of the tree to check its next entry M_2. Observe that $dist(q, M_2) < dist(q, o_{NN})$, so the node pointed by M_2 is visited. Node m_4 is also visited for the same reason, and after checking objects i, j, and k, we set $o_{NN} = k$ with distance $\sqrt{2}$. Entries m_5 and m_6 are further than $\sqrt{2}$ from q; thus, the corresponding nodes are not visited and the algorithm returns to the call for the root to examine M_3. Since entry M_3 is farther from q than its current NN, the subtree that it points to need not be visited and the algorithm terminates.

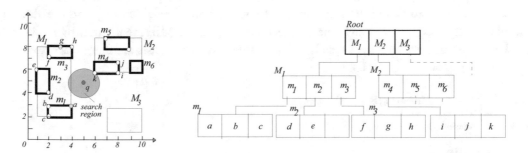

Figure 4.4: Example of nearest neighbor search using R–trees.

   Observe that with this method we have avoided examining large parts of the space; in fact, apart from the root, we only visited nodes M_1, M_2, m_1, and m_4. As an optimization for the DF_NN_search algorithm, we can examine the entries of a node in ascending order of their distance from q. For example, at the call $DF\_NN\_search(q, M_1, o_{NN})$, we first examine m_1, then m_3, and finally m_2. This brings two advantages. First, it is likely that we find a close neighbor of q that can prune the search space earlier. For instance, if we examined m_2 first, the nearest neighbor d found there could not help us prune m_1 or m_3. But, since we visit m_1 first, we are lucky to find a, which has larger pruning power since it is closer to q. The second advantage of ordering the entries in ascending order of their distance is that if we find an entry that we can prune, we immediately know that we can prune all other entries following it in the order. For instance, assume that we examine m_1, m_3, and m_2 in that order. After we find $o_{NN} = a$ in m_1, we can prune m_3, since $dist(q, m_3) \geq dist(q, o_{NN})$, as discussed. Also, since we know that $dist(q, m_3) \leq dist(q, m_2)$, we can immediately prune m_2 and any other entry after it in the order.

4.2.2   A BEST-FIRST NEAREST NEIGHBOR SEARCH ALGORITHM

Although the depth first search algorithm described above is quite efficient, it turns out that it does not access the minimum possible number of R–tree nodes at any problem instance. A more efficient branch-and-bound algorithm works in a manner between depth-first and breadth-first search and accesses the R–tree nodes in the most promising order of finding the nearest neighbor of the query object q. The idea is to maintain a heap (i.e., priority queue) Q that dynamically organizes visited R–tree node entries and objects with respect to their distance from q.

A pseudo-code for this *best-first* search algorithm (BF for short) is shown in Figure 4.5. Initially, Q contains all entries of the R–tree root; the top element of Q is the root entry whose MBR is the closest to the query object q. While there are still elements in the heap Q, the top element e with the minimum distance from q is accessed and removed from Q. If e is a non-leaf node entry, the node that is pointed by it is accessed and its contents are added to the heap. If e is a leaf node entry, then the object that is pointed by it is accessed from the spatial relation, its exact distance to q is computed and the object is added back to the heap. Finally, if the top element e of Q is an object, then this object is guaranteed to be the nearest neighbor of q and the algorithm terminates. The reason is that any object, object MBR, or node MBR that currently exists in the heap has larger distance to q than e, so it is not possible that there exists another object closer to q, according to Equations 4.1 and 4.2.

function BF_NN_search(object q, R–tree R): object o_{NN}
1.   initialize a priority queue Q;
2.   add all entries of R's root to Q;
3.   **while** not $empty(Q)$
4. $e := top(Q)$;
5.   remove e from Q;
6.   **if** e is a directory node entry **then**
7. $n :=$ R–tree node with address $e.ptr$;
8.   **for each** entry $e' \in n$
9.   add e' on Q;
10.   **else if** e is an entry of a leaf node **then**
11. $o :=$ object with address $e.ptr$;
12.   add o on Q;
13.   **else** /* e is an object */
14.   **return** $o_{NN} := e$;

Figure 4.5: Best-first nearest neighbor search using an R–tree.

To illustrate how BF works, consider again the example of Figure 4.4. Table 4.1 shows the heap contents at the beginning of each execution of the while loop. The numbers in the parentheses next to each content of Q correspond to the distance of the corresponding element to q. Initially, the three root entries and their distances from q are added to the heap. After M_1 (the top element of Q) is removed from the heap, BF accesses the node pointed by it and adds its entries to Q. This is repeated for M_2, the next entry on top of the heap. After this, m_4 becomes the top heap element, the corresponding node is visited and the object MBRs in it are added to the heap. The next entry to be de-heaped is k, which is an object MBR. The exact geometry $k.geom$ of the corresponding object is retrieved and en-heaped, using its distance to q as key. The next step retrieves $k.geom$ from the heap, which is an object, and the algorithm terminates reporting it as the nearest neighbor of q. Note that all remaining elements in the heap (MBRs of nodes, object MBRs, and objects) have distance to q greater than $\sqrt{2}$ (i.e., the distance between q and $k.geom$); therefore, they cannot contain or be the nearest neighbor. In this example, the objects are points, so the refinement step, where the object's geometry is accessed and the object is en-heaped again is not actually necessary. However, in the general case, the MBR-based distance of an object to q may vary significantly from the actual object's distance.

Table 4.1: Progress of BF in the example of Figure 4.4.	
Action	**Contents of Q after action**
initialization	$M_1(1), M_2(\sqrt{2}), M_3(\sqrt{8})$
de-heap M_1	$M_2(\sqrt{2}), m_1(\sqrt{5}), m_3(\sqrt{5}), M_3(\sqrt{8}), m_2(3)$
de-heap M_2	$m_4(\sqrt{2}), m_1(\sqrt{5}), m_3(\sqrt{5}), M_3(\sqrt{8}), m_2(3), m_5(\sqrt{13}), m_5(\sqrt{17})$
de-heap m_4	$k(\sqrt{2}), m_1(\sqrt{5}), M_3(\sqrt{5}), m_3(\sqrt{8}), m_2(3), i(\sqrt{10}), j(\sqrt{13}), m_5(\sqrt{13}), m_6(\sqrt{17})$
de-heap k	$k.geom(\sqrt{2}), m_1(\sqrt{5}), M_3(\sqrt{5}), m_3(\sqrt{8}), m_2(3), i(\sqrt{10}), j(\sqrt{13}), m_5(\sqrt{13}), m_6(\sqrt{17})$
de-heap $k.geom$	$m_1(\sqrt{5}), M_3(\sqrt{5}), m_3(\sqrt{8}), m_2(3), i(\sqrt{10}), j(\sqrt{13}), m_5(\sqrt{13}), m_6(\sqrt{17})$

Observe that this algorithm accesses fewer R–tree nodes compared to DF; only the root, M_1, M_2, and m_4 are accessed. In general, BF accesses only the R–tree nodes that intersect the *search region* centered at q with radius $dist(q, o_{NN})$, where o_{NN} is the actual NN of q. The search region for our example is the disk in gray color in Figure 4.4. In this sense, BF is an optimal algorithm, since it accesses only the necessary nodes of the R–tree.

4.2.3 k-NEAREST NEIGHBOR SEARCH AND INCREMENTAL SEARCH

How can we extend the DF and BF algorithms described above for the k-nearest neighbor search problem? The solution is simple. In DF, we just replace the current NN variable o_{NN} with a priority queue (i.e., a heap) H that maintains the nearest k neighbors found so far. In order to prune an entry, we need to compare it with the top element of H, corresponding to the farthest of the k nearest neighbors found so far. If a new object o is found that is closer to q than the top element of H, the top element is replaced by o and the heap H is updated (at a O($\log k$) cost). DF abandons search if it cannot find an entry closer to q than the top element of H. The modification of BF is even simpler. The algorithm, after retrieving the nearest neighbor, continues its operation until k (exact) objects have been de-heaped. These objects are the k nearest neighbors.

In *incremental* nearest neighbor search (often referred to as *distance browsing*), the user specifies a query point (or object) q and wants to retrieve all objects of a spatial relation R, in increasing order of their distance from q. The user can opt to stop search, when he is satisfied by the result obtained so far. As an application of this query assume that we wish to find the nearest city to our location, which has less than 10,000 inhabitants. If there are many such cities, it would be expensive to process the non-spatial selection ($R.population < 10,000$) before the nearest neighbor query. Thus, we could (incrementally) examine our nearest neighbors until we find one of small population. In general, distance browsing is a useful operator that generates a custom-based spatially sorted output incrementally.

The BF algorithm (described in Figure 4.5) can straightforwardly be used to solve the distance browsing problem. As in the k nearest neighbors query, we do not terminate as soon as we find the nearest neighbor. This time, we do not terminate even when k objects are output; the algorithm continues until the heap is empty: this would output all objects in increasing distance order to q. Thus, the BF algorithm can conveniently be implemented as an iterator that produces nearest neighbors incrementally and on-demand. On the other hand, the depth-first search algorithm cannot directly be modified for distance browsing, since it employs node pruning based on a bound from the current nearest neighbor(s).

When comparing the two methods DF and BF, one can say that BF is always superior, since it accesses the optimal number of nodes for NN search and is also appropriate for incremental NN search. However, a more careful look shows that there are cases where BF can perform worse than DF. This can happen if the system memory is too small to accommodate the queue Q. Note that DF, requires only one search path of the tree to fit in memory. On the other hand, since BF can expand more than one nodes at the same level (e.g., M_1 and M_2 in our example) before it goes to the next level, it usually has higher memory requirements. In hard problems, where the great majority of node MBRs have smaller distances to the query compared to the actual objects, the heap Q may exceed the memory size and in such cases DF may be preferable to BF. This case often happens in high-dimensional spaces where the distance between two random objects has a low variance and R–tree node MBRs tend to have large volumes.

4.3 SPATIAL JOINS

Spatial selections and nearest neighbor queries apply on a single spatial relation. *Spatial joins*, on the other hand, combine information from two relations based on a spatial predicate. An example of a spatial join query that we already illustrated in Figure 2.3 is "find all pairs of cities and rivers that intersect". Formally, given two spatial relations R and S and a spatial relationship θ, the spatial join $R \bowtie_\theta S$ is defined as $\{(r, s) : r \in R, s \in S, r \, \theta \, s\}$. During a spatial join, a relation may need to be scanned more than once and the super-linear cost of the operator renders its efficient processing of great importance.

Relational join methods are not directly applicable due to the special properties of spatial objects, as discussed in Section 2.3. A significant amount of research has been conducted toward the efficient processing of spatial joins. The first spatial join methods assumed that both inputs are indexed by some spatial access method (e.g., R–trees). Later, the database research focused on spatial join processing that does not solely rely on pre-existing indices. Such situations may arise when at least one input is an intermediate result of a preceding operator. Consider, for instance, the query "find all rivers of width larger than 20m, which intersect a forest". If there is a large percentage of narrow rivers, it might be natural to process the selection part of the query before the spatial join. In such an execution plan, even if there exists a spatial index on rivers, it is not employed by the join algorithm.

Table 4.2 classifies the spatial join techniques according to the assumption they make on pre-existing indices for the joined inputs. Methods of the first column can be applied only when both inputs are indexed (e.g., two relations Forests and Rivers are joined with respect to a spatial

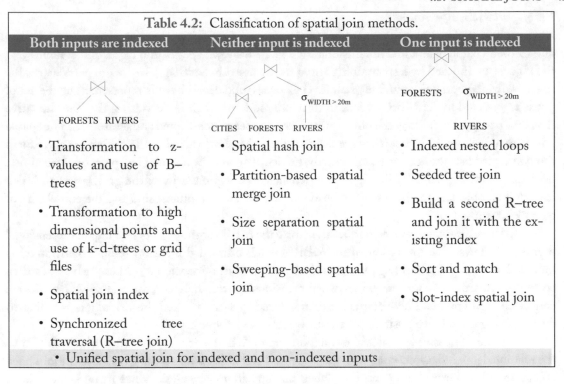

Table 4.2: Classification of spatial join methods.

Both inputs are indexed	Neither input is indexed	One input is indexed
• Transformation to z-values and use of B-trees	• Spatial hash join	• Indexed nested loops
• Transformation to high dimensional points and use of k-d-trees or grid files	• Partition-based spatial merge join	• Seeded tree join
• Spatial join index	• Size separation spatial join	• Build a second R-tree and join it with the existing index
• Synchronized tree traversal (R-tree join)	• Sweeping-based spatial join	• Sort and match
		• Slot-index spatial join
• Unified spatial join for indexed and non-indexed inputs		

predicate). Join algorithms in the second column can be used in cases when neither input is indexed (e.g., Forests that intersect some City are joined with Rivers wider than 20m). The third column includes algorithms suitable when only one input is indexed by an R–tree (e.g., Forests are joined with Rivers wider than 20m). Most of the spatial join techniques focus on the filter step of the query. The refinement step (i.e., testing the exact geometry of objects against the join predicate) is applied independently of the algorithm used for the filter step to the pairs that pass it, afterwards.

In the rest of this section, we describe the most important spatial join methods in each class and compare their relative performance. How the refinement step of a spatial join is processed will also be discussed. We will first confine our discussion on spatial join algorithms that can be applied when the join predicate θ is *intersects*. Next, we will briefly discuss how *distance* joins between point-sets or object-sets can be processed by extending methods for intersection joins.

4.3.1   INDEX-BASED METHODS

Spatial relations are often indexed by an access method (like the R–tree) that accelerates the processing of selection queries. Spatial join processing can take advantage of existing indices to direct search and prune many non-qualifying object pairs early.

Early spatial join algorithms

Most early spatial join algorithms apply transformation of objects in order to overcome difficulties due to their spatial extent and dimensionality. The first known spatial join algorithm assumes that the objects are indexed by a space filling curve, as discussed in Section 3.1.2. More particularly, the space is divided by a grid into fine granules (i.e., pixels) and each object is represented by the set of pixels intersected by its MBR, which, in turn, are modeled by the intervals on the Z-order curve that they occupy. Therefore, each object is modeled as a set of one-dimensional intervals. The spatial join is then performed in a sort-merge fashion; the object intervals of each relation are sorted and the two sorted lists are accessed concurrently, to identify pairs of intervals (i.e., pairs of objects) that overlap. The performance of the algorithm depends on the granularity of the grid; larger grids can lead to finer object approximations, but also increase the space requirements and the complexity of query evaluation.

Alternative spatial join techniques transform the MBRs of the objects into higher dimensional points as follows. The projection of an MBR to each original dimension (e.g., dimension x) is modeled as a pair of values (e.g., lower and upper bound in dimension x). These two values then correspond to a pair of coordinates in a two-dimensional space. Therefore, the original 2D MBRs are converted to 4D points. These points are then indexed by a grid file and the spatial join is evaluated by examining the relative positions of these objects in a systematic way.

A more aggressive spatial join evaluation approach is the spatial join index which, similar to the relational join index, pre-computes the join result and indexes it in order to retrieve the join pairs efficiently. This approach is appropriate when the data are mostly static (since its update overhead is non-negligible) and the join query is frequently applied.

The R–tree join

The R–tree join algorithm (RJ), often referred to as *tree matching* or *synchronous traversal*, computes the spatial join of two relations provided that they are both indexed by R–trees. RJ synchronously traverses both trees, starting from the roots and following entry pairs which intersect. Let n_R, n_S be two directory (non-leaf) nodes of the R–trees that index relations R and S, respectively. RJ is based on the following observation: if two entries $e_i \in n_R$ and $e_j \in n_S$ do not intersect, there can be no pair (o_R, o_S) of intersecting objects, where o_R and o_S are under the sub-trees pointed by e_i and e_j, respectively. A simple pseudo-code for RJ that outputs the result of the filter spatial join step (i.e., outputs pairs of objects whose MBRs intersect) is given in Figure 4.6. The pseudo-code assumes that both trees have the same height, yet it can be easily extended to the general case by applying range queries to the deeper tree when the leaf level of the shallow tree is reached.

Figure 4.7 illustrates two datasets indexed by R–trees. Initially, RJ is executed with the tree roots as parameters. The qualifying entry pairs at the root level are (A_1, B_1) and (A_2, B_2). Notice that since A_1 does not intersect B_2, there can be no object pairs under these entries that intersect. RJ is recursively called for the nodes pointed by the qualifying entries until the leaf level is reached, where the intersecting pairs (a_1, b_1) and (a_2, b_2) are output.

function RJ(Node n_R, Node n_S)
1.   **for each** $e_i \in n_R$
2.   **for each** $e_j \in n_S$, such that e_i.MBR $\cap$ e_j.MBR$\neq \emptyset$
3.   **if** n_R is a leaf node **then** /* n_S is also a leaf node */
4.   **output** $(e_i.ptr, e_j.ptr)$; /* a pair of object-ids passing the filter step */
5.   **else** /* n_R, n_S are directory nodes */
6. $RJ(e_i.ptr, e_j.ptr)$; /* run recursively for the nodes pointed by intersecting entries*/

Figure 4.6: A simplified version of the R–tree join algorithm.

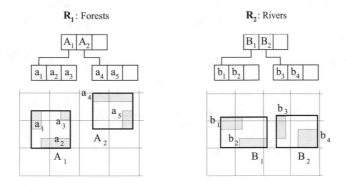

Figure 4.7: Two datasets indexed by R–trees.

Observe that every time the function RJ of Figure 4.6 is called, $|n_R| \cdot |n_S|$ pairs of entries are compared for intersection, where $|n|$ denotes the number of entries in a node n. This process is the computational burden of the algorithm, since it is repeated at every recursive call. We can use two simple heuristics to reduce the cost of this operation. The first optimization restricts the search space as follows. First, we linearly scan the entries $e_i \in n_R$ and prune those that do not intersect the MBR of n_S. Clearly, these entries cannot intersect any entry $e_j \in n_S$. For example, in Figure 4.8a, since entry r_i of node n_R does not intersect the MBR of node n_S, we know for sure that it cannot intersect any entry in n_S. Then we repeat the same process for the entries of n_S, by testing their intersection with n_R (this time s_j will be pruned among others from node n_S in Figure 4.8a). Thus the $\Theta(|n_R| \cdot |n_S|)$ cost of examining $|n_R| \cdot |n_S|$ pairs can be reduced to the cost of two linear scans, plus the cost of examining the pairs for all entries that were not pruned by this heuristic.

The second optimization heuristic is an adaptation of the *plane sweep* technique from Computational Geometry. The entries of n_R and n_S that survive the first pruning heuristic described above are sorted on one axis (e.g., x-axis), using the lower bounds of their projections there into two lists L_R, L_S. Then an (imaginary) *sweep line* perpendicular to the projection axis is initialized. The line is swept from $-\infty$ to ∞ visiting the entries of L_R and L_S in sorted order. Whenever a rectangle is met (e.g., $r_i \in L_R$) the line is anchored there and a loop is run to find the rectangles in the other list (e.g., L_S) that intersect it. These rectangles can only have their lower projection bound between the last position visited by the line in the corresponding list (e.g., L_S) and the upper bound of the anchored rectangle (e.g., r_i). A pseudo-code for this *forward sweep* technique is given in Figure 4.9.

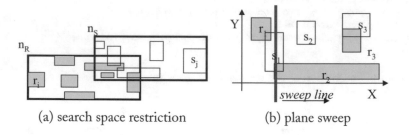

(a) search space restriction   (b) plane sweep

Figure 4.8: Computational optimizations in RJ.

function *Loop*(rectangle *anchor*, int *fpos*, *x*-axis sorted list of rectangles *L*)
1. $k := fpos$;
2.   **while** $(k \leq |L| \wedge L[k] \leq anchor.xu)$ /* *x*-intersection */
3.   **if** (*y-intersects*(*anchor*, *L[k]*)) **then** /* *y*-intersection */
4.   **output** (*anchor*, *L[k]*);
5. $k := k + 1$;

function *forward_sweep*(*x*-axis sorted lists of rectangles L_R, L_S)
1. $i := 1$; $j := 1$; /* point to the first elements of L_R, L_S */
2.   **while** $(i \leq |L_R| \wedge j \leq |L_S|)$
3.   **if** $(r_i.xl < s_j.xl)$ **then** /* r_i has smaller sort-key value than s_j */
4. $Loop(r_i, j, L_S)$;
5. $i := i + 1$;
6.   **else** /* s_j has smaller sort-key value than r_i */
7. $Loop(s_j, i, L_R)$;
8. $j := j + 1$;

Figure 4.9: The *forward sweep* heuristic employed by RJ.

4.3.2   ALGORITHMS THAT DO NOT CONSIDER INDEXES

The most straightforward and intuitive algorithm we can use to join two relations that are not indexed is *nested loops join*. This method can be applied for any type of joins (spatial, non-spatial) and condition predicates (topological, directional, distance, etc.). On the other hand, nested loops is the most expensive algorithm, since its cost is quadratic to the size of the relations (assuming that R and S have similar sizes). We can actually do much better. Spatial join algorithms for non-indexed inputs process the join in two steps; first the objects from both inputs are sorted and/or preprocessed using data structures and then these structures are used to quickly find objects that are in the same regions and intersect each other. The algorithms differ in the data structure they use and the way the data are preprocessed.

Spatial Hash Join

The *Spatial Hash Join* (SHJ) has common features with the relational hash-join algorithm. Set R is partitioned into K buckets; K is decided by system parameters and statistics about the data distribution, such that the expected number of objects hashed in a bucket would fit in memory. The initial extents of the buckets are determined by sampling. Each object is inserted into the bucket whose bounding box is enlarged the least after the insertion. Set S is hashed into buckets with the same extent as R's buckets, but with a different insertion policy; an object is inserted into all buckets that intersect it. Thus, some objects may go into more than one bucket (*replication*), and some may not be inserted at all (*filtering*). The algorithm does not always achieve partitions of equal number of objects from R, as sampling cannot guarantee the best possible slots. Equal sized partitions for S cannot be guaranteed in any case because the distribution of the objects in the two datasets may be totally different. Figure 4.10 shows an example of two sets of object MBRs, partitioned using SHJ. While distributing objects from R to three buckets (B_1^R to B_3^R), their extents are adjusted to become the MBRs of these objects (Figure 4.10a). The final extents of these buckets are used as fixed extents for the corresponding hash buckets of dataset S. Note that some objects from S are filtered and some are replicated during hashing.

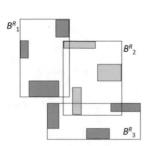 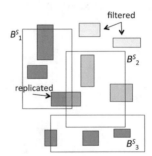

(a) Objects from set R in three buckets   (b) Hashing objects from set S

Figure 4.10: The partitioning phase of SHJ algorithm.

After hashing set S into buckets, the two bucket sets are joined; each bucket B_i^R from R is matched with the corresponding bucket B_i^S from S that covers the same spatial region. Similar to the relational hash join, for the join phase of SHJ, a single scan of both sets of buckets suffices, unless for some pair of buckets none of them fits in memory. If one bucket fits in memory, it is loaded and the objects of the other bucket are matched with it in a nested-loops fashion. If none of the buckets fits in memory, an R–tree is dynamically built for one of them, and the bucket-to-bucket join is executed in an indexed nested-loop fashion.

Partition Based Spatial Merge Join

Partition-Based Spatial Merge join (PBSM) is also based on the hash join paradigm. The space, in this case, is regularly partitioned using an orthogonal grid and objects from both datasets are hashed into partitions corresponding to grid cells, replicating wherever necessary. Figure 4.11a illustrates a regular space partitioning incurred by PBSM and some data hashed into the partitions. Objects hashed into the same partitions are then joined in memory using plane sweep. If the data inserted in a partition do not fit in memory, the algorithm recursively repartitions the cell into smaller parts and redistributes the objects. Since data from both datasets may be replicated to multiple partitions, the output of the algorithm has to be sorted in order to remove pairs reported more than once. Reporting of duplicates can be avoided by a simple technique, which outputs the intersected pair of objects only if the geometric centroid of their intersection area falls inside the current partition. This way, a pair of objects, which are replicated into two partitions and they are detected to overlap in both of them, is considered only once in the join result.

When the data to be joined are skewed, some partitions may contain a large percentage of the hashed objects, whereas others would have very few objects, rendering the algorithm inefficient. In order to evenly distribute the data in the partitions and efficiently handle skewed data, a spatial hash function is introduced. The cells of the grid are assigned to partitions according to this function and the space covered by a partition is no longer continuous, but consists of a number of scattered tiles. Figure 4.11b shows such a (round-robin like) spatial hash function. For example, partition 1 consists of six tiles scattered around the space.

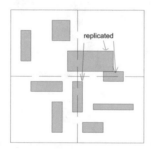
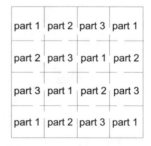

(a) four partitions and a set of hashed objects   (b) a spatial hash function

Figure 4.11: Regular partitioning by PBSM.

Size Separation Spatial Join
Another algorithm that applies regular partitioning, like PBSM, but avoids object replication is *Size Separation Spatial join* (S^{3}J). S^{3}J uses a hierarchical space decomposition. L partition layers of progressively larger resolution are introduced; the layer at level l partitions the space into $4l$ cells. A rectangle is then assigned to the topmost layer where it is not intersected by a grid line. This method achieves separation of the data according to their size. The rectangles in each layer are then sorted according to the Hilbert space filling curve value of their MBR's center. A synchronized scan of the layer files is finally performed and the rectangles from dataset R in a partition at level l are joined with all partitions of dataset S that intersect it at levels $0, \ldots, l$. A partition from S is joined with

partitions from R at levels $0, \ldots, l - 1$. The Hilbert values of the data inside a layer determine the order of the join, avoiding scanning a partition more than once. Figure 4.12 shows two partition layers of both datasets. Partition $r_{2,3}$ is joined with $s_{2,3}$ and $s_{1,0}$, and partition $s_{2,3}$ is joined with $r_{1,0}$.

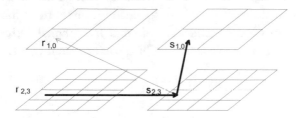

Figure 4.12: Size Separation Spatial Join.

S^3J also maintains a dynamic spatial bitmap which, after partitioning the first set, indicates the cells at each layer that contain at least one rectangle, or cover same area with cells at other layers that contain at least one rectangle. This bitmap can be used during the partitioning of the second set to filter entries that cannot intersect any rectangle of the first set. If a rectangle from set S is to be hashed into a partition cell and the bitmap entry of the cell is zero, the hashed rectangle is filtered out.

Scalable Sweeping-Based Spatial Join
Scalable Sweeping-based Spatial Join (SSSJ) is a relatively simple algorithm that is based on plane sweep. Both datasets are sorted according to the lower bound of their projection on an axis (e.g., the x-axis) and some variant of plane sweep (e.g., the *forward-sweep* algorithm described in Section 4.3.1) is applied to compute the intersecting pairs. SSSJ is based on the square-root rule: the expected number of rectangles in a dataset R that intersect the sweep line is $\sqrt{|R|}$, where $|R|$ is the total number of rectangles in R. SSSJ initiates an internal memory plane sweep algorithm. If it runs out of memory, i.e., the rectangles intersected by the sweep line do not fit in memory, the space is dynamically partitioned by stripes parallel to the sorted axis, the rectangles are hashed into the stripes, and plane sweep is recursively executed for each stripe.

4.3.3   SINGLE-INDEX JOIN METHODS

Methods in this class can be applied when one input is indexed but the other is not. Such situations often arise when processing complex queries, where another operator precedes the spatial join; in this case, index-based methods cannot directly be applied, because the intermediate result is not supported by any index. Also, algorithms that consider non-indexed inputs could be expensive. All single-index join methods were proposed after RJ, and they assume that the indexed input is supported by an R–tree. Most of them build a second structure for the non-indexed input and match it with the existing tree.

Indexed Nested Loops Join

In accordance to the equivalent algorithm for relational joins, *Indexed Nested Loops Join* (INLJ) applies a window query to the existing R–tree for each rectangle from the non-indexed set. This method can be efficient only when the non-indexed input is very small. Otherwise, the large number of selection queries can incur excessive computational overhead and access a large number of index pages.

Seeded Tree Join

Let R be a dataset indexed by an R–tree and S be a non-indexed dataset. The *Seeded Tree Join* algorithm (STJ) builds an R–tree for S, using the existing R–tree for R as a seed, and then applies RJ (Section 4.3.1) to match them. The rationale behind creating a *seeded* R–tree for the second input, instead of a normal R–tree, is the fact that if the new tree has similar high-level node extents with the R–tree of R, this would lead to minimization of overlapping node pairs during tree matching. Thus, the seeded tree construction algorithm creates an R–tree which is optimal for the spatial join and not for range searching. The seeded tree construction is divided into two phases: the *seeding* phase and the *growing* phase. At the seeding phase, the top k levels (k is a parameter of the algorithm) of the existing R–tree are copied to formulate the top k levels of the new R–tree for S. The entries in the lowest of these levels are called *slots*. After copying, the slots maintain the copied extent, but they point to empty (null) sub-trees. During the growing phase, all objects from S are inserted into the seeded tree. A rectangle is inserted under the slot that contains it, or needs the least area enlargement. Figure 4.13 shows an example of a seeded tree structure. The top $k = 2$ levels of the existing R–tree are copied to guide the insertion of the second dataset.

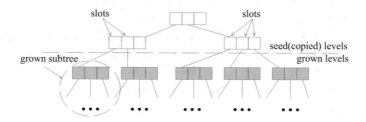

Figure 4.13: A seeded tree.

Some heuristics can be used to minimize the cost of this algorithm. First, if an object from S does not intersect the region of any slot, then it can be *filtered out*, since it cannot intersect any object from R. We can also reduce the I/O cost, by postponing the construction of the tree. For each slot, we can introduce a *hash bucket* and hash the objects under it. Thus, the objects which are to be inserted under a slot are written in a temporary file. After all objects are inserted, a (sub-)R–tree is constructed for each temporary file, and is pointed at by the corresponding slot in the seeded tree. In order to implement this mechanism and minimize random I/O accesses, at least one page in the memory buffer should be allocated for each slot. If the buffer is full, all slots that have more than a constant number of pages flush their data to disk and memory is freed. A problem with STJ, however, is that it cannot directly be applied under limited memory conditions. In order for the above algorithm to work efficiently, the number of slots (K) should not exceed the number of pages (M) in the system buffer. If $K > M$, it is not possible to allocate one memory page for each slot and hashing can be very expensive. Thus the algorithm is inefficient when the fanout of the R–tree nodes is large and the memory buffer is relatively small. Consider, for instance, a dataset of 100,000 objects which are indexed by a 8K page size R–tree. Under the assumption that each node entry is 20 bytes long (16 for the x- and y-coordinates, plus 4 for the object id or node reference), the capacity of a tree node is 409; thus, the dataset can be indexed by a 2-level R–tree, with 245 leaf nodes and 1 root. When applying STJ, we have to copy the root level of the R–tree to the seeded tree, which results in $K = 245$. As a consequence, in this example, the algorithm cannot be applied for buffers smaller than 1.96Mbytes.

Build and Match

Building a packed R–tree using bulk loading can be much more efficient in terms of both CPU time and I/O than constructing it incrementally. Moreover, packed R–trees have minimum number of nodes and height and could be very efficient for range queries and spatial joins. The *Build and Match* (BaM) method first builds a packed R–tree for the non-indexed dataset S and then joins it with the existing tree of R, using RJ.

Sort and Match

Sort and Match (SaM) is an alternative of BaM that avoids building a whole R–tree structure prior to matching. The algorithm employs the STR bulk-loading technique (see Section 3.3.3) to sort the rectangles from the non-indexed dataset S, but instead of building the packed tree, it matches each in-memory created leaf node with the leaf nodes from the R–tree of R that intersect it, using the structure of the tree to guide search. For each produced leaf node n_L at the last phase of STR, a window query using the MBR of n_L is applied on R's tree, in order to identify the leaf nodes there that intersect n_L. Plane sweep is then applied to match n_L with the qualifying leaves of R's tree. The matching phase of SaM is expected to be efficient, as two consecutive produced nodes will be close to each other with high probability and there will be good utilization of the LRU buffer. Graphical illustrations of BaM and SaM are shown in Figure 4.14.

Slot Index Spatial Join

Slot Index Spatial Join (SISJ) is a hash-based spatial join algorithm, which combines ideas from STJ and SHJ. SISJ uses the existing R–tree to define a set of hash buckets. If K is the desired number of

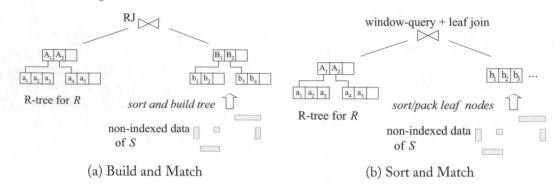

(a) Build and Match   (b) Sort and Match

Figure 4.14: Algorithms based on bulk-loading.

partitions (tuned according to the available memory), SISJ first finds the topmost level of the tree such that the number of entries there is larger than or equal to K. These entries are then grouped into K (possibly overlapping) partitions called *slots* . Each slot contains the MBR of the indexed R–tree entries, along with a list of pointers to these entries. Figure 4.15 illustrates a 3-level R–tree (the leaf level is not shown) and a slot index built over it. If $K = 9$, the root level contains too few entries to be used as partition buckets. As the number of entries in the next level is over K, they are partitioned in 9 (for this example) slots. The grouping policy used by SISJ is based on the R*–tree insertion algorithm. After building the slot index, all objects from the non-indexed relation are hashed into buckets with the same extents as the slots. If an object does not intersect with any bucket, it is filtered; if it intersects more than one bucket, it is replicated. The join phase of SISJ loads all data from the R–tree under a slot and joins them (in memory) with the corresponding hash-bucket from the non-indexed dataset (in a similar way as SHJ).

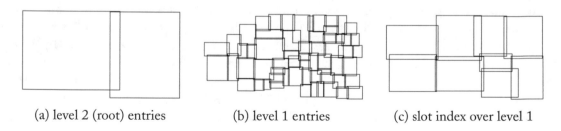

(a) level 2 (root) entries   (b) level 1 entries   (c) slot index over level 1

Figure 4.15: Entries of an R–tree and a slot index built over them.

4.3.4   A UNIFIED SPATIAL JOIN APPROACH

So far, we have differentiated between the cases of index support for neither, one, or both spatial join inputs. Most discussed methods partition the non-indexed data somehow and then join them using any indexes that may exist. The SSSJ algorithm, which applies external-memory plane-sweep, uses a different logic, since it does not rely on partitioning. This method can be extended to a *Unified Spatial Join* (USJ) approach, which performs the join independently to whether the data are indexed or not by R-trees. If neither input is indexed, USJ behaves exactly like SSSJ, i.e., it externally sorts the datasets and applies plane sweep. If any of the datasets are indexed, instead of externally sorting them, USJ accesses the data in it in sorted order with the help of a priority queue, which traverses the tree nodes and entries in them in the plane sweep order. This way, sorting is avoided and the existing tree is used to guide the incremental access of the objects indexed by it in sorted order.

4.3.5   COMPARISON OF SPATIAL JOIN ALGORITHMS

Since indexes can facilitate the spatial join operation, algorithms (like RJ) that are based on existence of indexes are typically more efficient (at least in terms of CPU) compared to methods that do not rely on indexes. For example, RJ (which joins two R–trees) is expected to be more efficient than SISJ (which uses one R–tree), which is expected to be more efficient than SHJ (which does not use trees). In terms of I/O, methods that rely on hashing (e.g., SHJ and SISJ) access fewer pages compared to sort-based approaches (e.g., SSSJ); still the latter are more I/O efficient in practice if the difference between random and sequential I/Os is considered. In this case, the unified approach (USJ), which is based on sequential scanning, may even outperform RJ, which does not focus on ordered accessing of the tree nodes. Methods that use partitions of fixed spatial extents, like PBSM, are suitable for processing multiple joins in parallel, since the space partitions (and the local joins for them) can be assigned to different processors.

4.3.6   THE REFINEMENT STEP OF A SPATIAL JOIN

The spatial join algorithms presented already focus on the efficient processing of the filter step of the spatial join. Nevertheless, efficient processing of the refinement step is also important, especially when the number of candidate object pairs that pass the filter step is large. The refinement step is actually part of multi-step process that aims at minimizing the object pairs for which the expensive geometric intersection test has to be applied. For each object apart from its MBR, two more approximations are stored; a conservative and a progressive approximation. An example of a *conservative* approximation is the *convex hull*, whereas a good *progressive* approximation is the *maximum enclosed rectangle* (MER) (see Figure 4.16).

After the filter step, for each candidate pair, the conservative and progressive approximations of the objects are tested for intersection. If the conservative approximations of two objects do not intersect, the object pair is pruned (false hit). If the progressive approximations of two objects intersect, the exact objects definitely intersect. In all other cases no conclusive result can be drawn and the exact geometry of the objects is tested for intersection at the final step of the algorithm. Figure 4.17 illustrates this 3-step spatial join processing methodology (assuming that the filter step is processed by RJ).

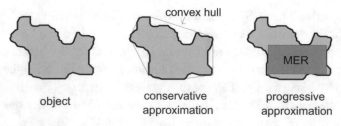

Figure 4.16: An object and two approximations.

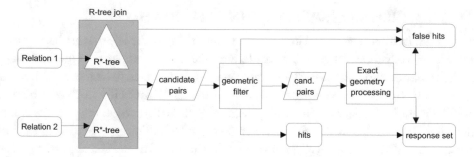

Figure 4.17: Multi-step processing of spatial joins.

An alternative object approximation that reduces the number of candidate pairs to be tested during the refinement step of spatial joins is to define and store for each object a *signature* that captures a raster approximation of the object and replaces any conservative and progressive approximations. A 4-color raster grid that covers the object's area is defined. If the object does not cover any part of a cell, the corresponding cell value is set to 0 (empty). If the object covers less than 50% of a cell, the cell value is set to 1 (weak). If the coverage is more than 50%, the cell value is set to 2 (strong). Finally, if the cell is totally covered, its value is set to 3 (full). Figure 4.18 shows a raster approximation example. For each candidate pair the common object cells are compared and conclusions are drawn about the intersection of the objects. For instance if a pair of full or strong cells is found then the objects definitely intersect, whereas if all the common cells are empty for some object then the pair is a false hit. In some cases, e.g., when some cells are both weak or there is one weak and one strong cell, no conclusion can be drawn and the object pair remains a candidate hit requiring an exact geometry test.

4.3.7   DISTANCE JOINS AND RELATED QUERIES

Given two relations R, S and a distance threshold ϵ, the *distance join*, returns object pairs $\langle r, s \rangle, r \in R$, $s \in S$, such that $dist(r, s) \leq \epsilon$. An example of such a query is "find pairs of hotels and restaurants which are within at most distance ϵ from each other".

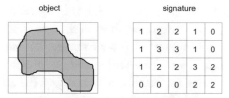

Figure 4.18: An object and its raster approximation (signature).

Research on the *distance join* operator has mainly focused on point datasets because they are more relevant in applications of higher dimensionality (e.g., image similarity retrieval, data mining), where the data are points. If two points r and s are within distance ϵ, then the circles d_r, d_s with centers r, s and radii $\epsilon/2$ intersect, implying that their MBRs r' and s' intersect, as illustrated in Figure 4.19a. Therefore, given two point sets R and S that fit in memory, we can reduce the $O(|R||S|)$ distance join cost, by applying a plane-sweep algorithm on the MBRs of their circles. Then, we remove any false hits (like the one in Figure 4.19b) by exact distance calculations. Notice that point extension can be performed dynamically and on-demand for each value of ϵ, without any precomputations. Figure 4.19c shows how this method can be generalized for R–tree MBRs (i.e., for the R–tree join algorithm), which are extended to *Minkowski* regions and approximated by rectangles. An alternative method, which simplifies the join, is to extend by ϵ and approximate only the points (and MBRs) of one dataset.

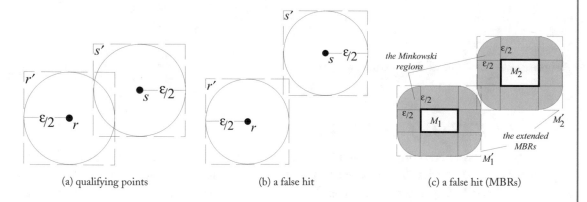

(a) qualifying points   (b) a false hit   (c) a false hit (MBRs)

Figure 4.19: Point and MBR extensions for distance join processing.

Using these properties, we can extend spatial intersection join algorithms to process distance joins, by (dynamically) extending the MBRs of index nodes (or hash buckets). The spatial distance join also has some interesting variants. A *closest pairs query*, given a parameter k, returns the set of k closest pairs $CP=\{(r, s) : r \in R, s \in S\}$, such that $dist(r, s) \leq dist(r', s')$, for all $r' \in R, s' \in$

$S : (r', s') \notin CP$. A similar (non-commutative) operator is the *all k-nearest neighbors query*, which returns for each object from R, its k nearest neighbors in S. Note that these two queries combine the spatial join with the nearest neighbor query. A more complex join variant is the *iceberg distance join*, which, given two datasets R and S, a real number ϵ, and an integer t, retrieves all pairs of objects from R and S such that (i) the pairs are within distance ϵ, and (ii) an object of R appears at least t times in the distance join result (e.g., "find all hotels that are close to at least 10 restaurants").

As an example for the spatial join variants, consider Figure 4.20, which illustrates a set of hotels $\{h_1, h_2, h_3\}$ and a set of restaurants $\{r_1, r_2, r_3, r_4, r_5\}$. The ϵ-distance join between these two sets returns seven pairs: (h_1, r_1), (h_1, r_2), (h_2, r_2), (h_2, r_3), (h_2, r_4), (h_3, r_4), and (h_3, r_5). The 3-closest pairs are (h_2, r_3), (h_3, r_5), and (h_3, r_4). The all 1-nearest neighbor operator (for the hotels) returns (h_1, r_2), (h_2, r_3), and (h_3, r_5) — note that ϵ is not involved in closest pairs and all k-nearest neighbors operations. Finally, the iceberg distance join for $t=3$ returns (h_2, r_2), (h_2, r_3), and (h_2, r_4) — observe that h_2 is the only hotel with at least 3 nearby restaurants. A number of algorithms that extend techniques for spatial joins and nearest neighbor search have been developed to process these interesting distance join variants.

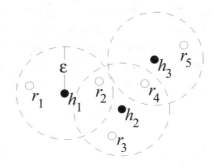

Figure 4.20: Example of distance join variants.

4.4   QUERY OPTIMIZATION

The query optimizer is an important module of a DBMS. Given a complex query q, the role of the optimizer is to (i) reorder the operators of q and (ii) select appropriate evaluation algorithms for each operator, in order to minimize the expected evaluation cost of the query. In other words, the query optimizer determines a good *query evaluation plan*. Relational query optimizers typically push selections and projections as low as possible in the tree that defines the order of query operations (i.e., the query evaluation tree). The optimal order for the operators is determined with the use of a dynamic programming algorithm (often combined with heuristics to reduce the cost of estimating the optimal plan). The query optimization algorithm relies on the existence of (i) statistics about the data distribution and the structure of existing indexes and (ii) accurate models that estimate the cost and selectivity (i.e., output size) of the involved operations in the query, based on the statistics.

The involvement of spatial data and spatial query operations in database queries affects the query optimizer. Together with the relational operations, the optimizer has to consider the spatial operations that may appear in queries. Let us see a concrete example to understand the implication of spatial data in query optimization. Consider the query: "find all cities of population at least 20,000, which are crossed by any river that intersects Germany". The query has two selections (one non-spatial selection on cities and one spatial selection on rivers), one spatial join (cities with rivers) and one projection (cities). The order by which the operations are evaluated, as well as the choice of evaluation algorithms for them affects the cost of the overall query evaluation. Assuming that the two relations (cities and rivers) are spatially indexed by R–trees, Figure 4.21 shows two of the possible evaluation plans for the query. The left plan applies the selections as early as possible in order to reduce the input size of the join. However, since the results of the selections are no longer indexed, a spatial join algorithm that does not rely on indexes should be used (e.g., PBSM), at higher expected cost compared to index-based algorithms. The plan on the right of the figure chooses to apply the spatial selection after the join and uses a spatial join algorithm that exploits the R–tree for the Rivers relation (e.g., SISJ). The cost of each plan can be estimated by expected costs and selectivities of the involved operations. For example, if most rivers in the relation are expected to qualify the spatial selection, then the plan on the right could be better than the plan on the left.

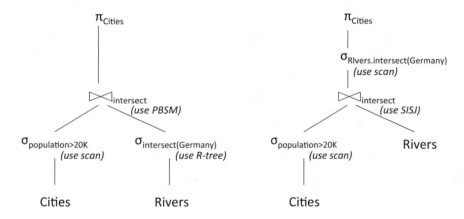

Figure 4.21: Two evaluation plans.

There is a significant body of work on estimating the selectivity and cost of spatial operations. Estimates depend on the existence of statistics, so defining and using good statistical approaches that summarize the data distribution and the properties of spatial indexes is important.

4.4.1   SELECTIVITY ESTIMATION

To estimate the selectivity of a spatial selection, we need statistics about the spatial distribution of the objects in the queried relation. A simple approach is to consider only simple, global statistics and assume that the objects are uniformly distributed. For example, consider a set of N uniformly distributed points in a rectangular region U. The estimated number of points included in the spatial range Q of a query is simply $\frac{area(Q)}{area(U)} \times N$; i.e., the total number of points multiplied by the fraction of the spatial domain occupied by the query range. If the spatial relation contains extended objects instead of points, in addition to their cardinality N, we use the average projection lengths of the object MBRs in each dimension. If we assume uniformity of object sizes in each dimension, then we can model a spatial selection query Q on the objects as an extended query Q' on point data. The extent of Q' in each dimension is extended by the average projection length of object MBRs there. Figure 4.22a shows a set of uniformly distributed rectangles, which all have nearly equal projection lengths in each dimension. The range query, modeled by the dashed square in the figure is equivalent to the query illustrated in Figure 4.22b, if we model each object as the left-upper corner point of the corresponding rectangle. Therefore, the selectivity of the original query can be estimated by $\frac{area(Q')}{area(U)} \times N$. In practice, neither the spatial objects in a relation are uniformly distributed in the spatial domain nor their MBRs have equal projection lengths at each dimension. Therefore, more detailed statistics are necessary in order to derive accurate selectivity estimates.

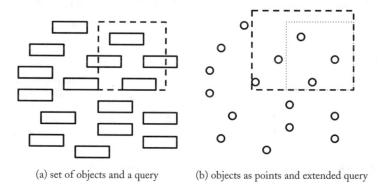

(a) set of objects and a query   (b) objects as points and extended query

Figure 4.22: Reducing extended objects to points for selectivity estimation.

Spatial histograms

Histograms are statistical summaries, which have been widely used in database systems to facilitate query optimization. For relational data, a histogram divides the value domain of an attribute into ranges; for each range, the total number of tuples in the relation is recorded in the histogram. Therefore, the histogram is a vector of value ranges with the total number of tuples in each range. A value range is often called a *bucket*. For example, consider an Employees relation and a histogram on the Age attribute of the relation. The histogram could be $\{\langle[18, 30), 25\rangle, \langle[30, 40), 34\rangle, \langle[40, 50), 13\rangle, \langle[50, 70], 7\rangle\}$, summarizing that there 25 employees of ages between 18 and 30, etc.

Histograms are used to estimate the selectivity of selections. For this purpose, the distribution of tuples that fall in a bucket is assumed to be uniform. Given a selection range (e.g., age between 25 and 45), the number of tuples that fall in it is estimated by adding the counts of buckets that are contained in the query range (e.g., 34 for bucket [30, 40)) to the counts of buckets that partially overlap the query interval, multiplied by the fraction of the overlap (e.g., $25 \times \frac{25-18}{30-18}$ for bucket [18, 30) and $13 \times \frac{45-40}{50-40}$ for bucket [40, 50)).

The higher the number of buckets used to define a histogram, the higher the expected accuracy of the histogram, but also the higher the overhead to store and update it. Given a desired number of buckets B, there are several ways to define a histogram. An *equi-width* histogram defines buckets of equal ranges. An *equi-depth* histogram divides the value domain in a way such that all buckets have the same aggregate count. A *V-optimal* histogram divides buckets in a way, such that the expected error in selectivity estimation is minimized.

Histograms can also be used for spatial selectivity estimation. For example, consider a set of two-dimensional points, modeling the locations of cities on a city map. We can partition the city map into regions (e.g., with the help of a grid) and then count the number of cities within each region. Given a spatial selection range, to estimate its selectivity, we can accumulate the counts of regions included in the range and add the fractional counts of regions that partially overlap with it. If the objects are not points, then in each bucket b_i, together with the number of objects whose centroid falls inside b_i, we store the average extent of object MBRs in each dimension that are assigned in the bucket. To estimate the output size of a range query, in this case, for the partially overlapped buckets, the query range is extended in each dimension by half the average extent of the objects in the corresponding bucket.

Spatial histogram construction

The problem of defining good histogram buckets for spatial data is not as easy as in the case of relational data. First, the spatial data domain is two-dimensional; in this case, the problem of finding an optimal set of bucket ranges that minimizes the selectivity estimation error is NP-hard. The reason is the exponential number of possible partitions of the spatial domain into buckets. The extent of spatial objects add to the complexity of this problem; there can be skew both in the locations and the sizes of extent in the distribution of objects in space. Therefore, heuristics for defining partitions have been considered, such that the distribution of locations and sizes of the objects that fall in each bucket is as uniform as possible.

Within a bucket, measuring the skew of object locations and sizes can be done with the help of a *spatial density* measure. The spatial density of any point in space is the number of object MBRs that contain that point. The *spatial skew* $s(b_i)$ of a bucket b_i is then the statistical variance of the spatial densities of all points in b_i. The spatial skew of an entire space partitioning into m buckets is then the weighted sum of the spatial skews of all buckets: $\sum_1^m n_i s(b_i)$, where n_i is the number of objects assigned to bucket b_i.

Given a desired number of buckets B, finding the optimal space partitioning into disjoint bucket regions that has the minimum spatial skew is an NP-hard problem. Min-Skew is a greedy heuristic, which efficiently finds a partitioning of low spatial skew. The idea is to first partition the space, using a regular grid, into cells[2] and compute for each cell its *spatial density*, as the number of object MBRs that intersect with the cell. The grid is then iteratively partitioned into buckets, by choosing each time the bucket split that results in the greatest reduction in the spatial skew. That is, initially we consider a single bucket containing all cells and find the axis-parallel split that maximizes the spatial-skew reduction if we use the split to replace the bucket by two new buckets. The process is iteratively repeated for the resulting buckets until B buckets are generated.

Selectivity estimation for spatial joins

To estimate the selectivity of a spatial join between relations R and S, we can simulate the join as a sequence of selection queries to relation S, one for each object from R. By summing the expected output sizes of all selection queries, we get an estimate for the join output size. Under the assumption that the location and size distributions of objects in the spatial relations are uniform, the output size of the join can be estimated by $|R| \times |S| \times \frac{r_x + s_x}{u_x} \times \frac{r_y + s_y}{u_y}$, where r_i and s_i are the average projection lengths of the object MBRs in dimension i ($i \in \{x, y\}$) for relations R and S, respectively, and u_i is the length of the spatial domain in dimension i. For example, quantity $\frac{r_x + s_x}{u_x}$ reflects the chance that a random pair of object MBRs from R and S intersect in the x dimension. Note that if $\frac{r_i + s_i}{u_i} > 1$, for any $i \in \{x, y\}$, the corresponding quantity is replaced by 1 in the selectivity estimation formula.

If spatial histograms for the two relations are available, then the formula is applied for each pair of buckets that intersect. The common intersection area of the buckets is used for defining u_x and u_y and $|R|$, $|S|$ are replaced by the number of objects from each relation, which are expected to have their geometric centroid inside this area.

4.4.2 COST ESTIMATION FOR SPATIAL QUERY OPERATIONS

Besides selectivity estimation, the second essential tool for query optimization is estimating the cost of the involved operations in the query. Unlike selectivity, the cost of an operation depends on the technique which is used to implement it. For the three main spatial query operations (selection, nearest neighbor search, and spatial joins), we now discuss models for their cost estimation.

Cost of spatial selections

If a spatial selection is applied on data that are not spatially indexed, then the cost is proportional to the size of the queried relation, since the selection is implemented by scanning the whole relation in this case. The presence of a spatial index reduces this cost. To estimate the cost (in terms of I/O accesses) of a spatial selection issued on an R–tree, we employ statistics about the sizes and distribution of the MBRs in non-leaf node entries.

[2]The number of cells should be much larger than B but small enough for them and their statistics to fit in memory.

The expected number of R–tree nodes accessed by a spatial selection is equal to the expected number of non-leaf MBRs that intersect the query plus the access of the R-tree root. Therefore, the I/O cost estimation is reduced to a selectivity estimation problem for the non-leaf tree entries. In specific, let L be the number of R–tree levels. Let N_l be the total number of entries in nodes at R–tree level l and $r_{i,l}$ the average length of the MBRs of these entries at dimension i. The cost of a window query, assuming that the entries at each level of the tree are uniformly distributed can then be estimated by $1 + \sum_{l=1}^{L-1} \Pi_{i \in \{x,y\}} \min\{1, \frac{r_{i,l}+q_i}{u_i}\}$, where q_i (u_i) is the projection length of the query (the entire spatial domain) at dimension i (assuming a rectangular query). Therefore, cost estimation of selection queries over R–trees is done by keeping track of statistics about the number of entries and their average sizes at each tree level. The cost for non-uniform datasets can be computed with the aid of histograms that summarize the distribution of MBRs at the different levels of the R–tree.

Cost of nearest neighbor search

We did not discuss the selectivity of k nearest neighbor (k-NN) search, because it is trivially determined by the query parameter k. The cost of a k-NN query depends on the expected circular area, within which all objects have to be accessed during the query. In other words, the cost of a k-NN search (if the best-first search algorithm is applied) is equivalent to the cost of a circular range query around the query point q; the circle is the minimum one that contains k objects. Thus, to derive a cost model for k-NN search, we first have to estimate the distance D_k between q and the k-th nearest neighbor.

A simple way to estimate D_k is to assume a uniform data distribution and that the search circle is enclosed by the spatial domain. In this case, the expected number of objects that fall in a circle of radius r is $\frac{\pi r^2}{area(U)} \times N$, i.e., the probability that a random point falls in the circle is the ratio between the area enclosed by the circle and the total area of the spatial domain U. Therefore, D_k can be estimated by setting this quantity equal to k and solving by r: i.e., $D_k = r = \sqrt{\frac{k \times area(U)}{N\pi}}$. In practice, however, the search circle may partially fall outside the spatial domain (e.g., if the query point q is close to the boundary, or in higher dimensional spaces); therefore, such *boundary effects* should be considered in this case. If the data are non-uniform, histogram techniques are used in combination with the consideration of the boundary effects. After estimating D_k and the search area of the query, the problem is reduced to estimating the cost of a (circular) range query, which can be done by extending the methodology for rectangular range queries, described above.

Cost of spatial joins

For the R–tree spatial join algorithm (RJ), the cost estimation procedure follows a similar logic as the cost estimation for spatial selections using R–trees. Recall that the algorithm follows recursively pairs of MBRs at each level of the tree that intersect each other. Therefore, the number of node accesses at a certain level of the joined R–trees can be estimated by the number of MBR pairs from the two trees at the previous level that intersect. Therefore, for two relations R and S, both indexed by R–trees, the spatial join cost can be estimated by $2 + 2 \times \sum_{l=1}^{L-1} N_{R,l} \times N_{S,l} \times \Pi_{i \in \{x,y\}} \min\{1, \frac{r_{i,l}+s_{i,l}}{u_i}\}$. Here, $N_{R,l}$ ($N_{S,l}$) is the total number of entries in nodes of the R–tree that indexes R (S), at level l, $r_{i,l}$ ($s_{i,l}$) is the average projection length of these entries at dimension i, and u_i is the projection length of the spatial domain at dimension i. The formula expresses that apart from the two tree roots that have to be accessed, at each level of the tree (except from the leaves level), each intersecting pair of entries will cause two node accesses at the level below. The formula assumes uniform data and can be adapted with the help of histograms for other distributions. In addition, it assumes that each node access corresponds to an I/O access, which is not reasonable, as systems typically employ memory buffers to store and reuse recently accessed pages. Therefore, in practice, when counting I/Os, the number of expected accesses for a given node is discounted using the probability that the node already resides in memory.

For other join algorithms, the I/O cost is estimated following the details of the algorithm. Join algorithms come with a pre-processing cost (i.e., for generating partitions or sorting) and a join cost. For example, the cost of SISJ includes (i) the cost for reading the top-most levels of the R–tree that indexes the first relation R to determine the slot index, (ii) the cost of hashing the non-indexed relation S to partitions according to the slot index, (iii) the cost of accessing the subtrees in R under each slot and joining it with the corresponding partition from S. Thus, the R–tree nodes of R are accessed only once, while the data from S are accessed three times; once for partitioning into buckets based on the slots, once for writing these buckets to the disk, and once for reading the partitions and joining them with the corresponding data from R. The use of buffering again can significantly reduce the number of necessary I/O accesses for S.

4.5   SUMMARY

The efficient evaluation of spatial query operations is a core requirement of a spatial database system. Query evaluation algorithms consider using potential spatial indexes whenever they exist and they are usable. Since spatial access methods are designed for the efficient evaluation of spatial selections, query evaluation techniques for such queries straightforwardly perform data accesses, directed by the index structure. In this chapter, we considered the R–tree as the presumed spatial access method and discussed algorithms designed for this index.

k nearest neighbor search is performed by modifying spatial selection search. The depth-first algorithm traverses the R–tree in a depth-first fashion and maintains in a heap the k nearest objects found so far. The farthest object in the heap defines a bound; whenever an encountered R–tree entry is farther than the current k-th nearest neighbor, the entry and the sub-tree pointed by it are pruned. The best-first algorithm operates in a slightly different fashion. The entries of the tree, starting from the root entries, are added to a priority queue and accessed in the order defined by their distance to the query object. Whenever an entry is accessed from the top of the queue, the node entries or the object pointed by it are accessed and enheaped. The first k objects to be de-heaped during the algorithm are query results. The best-first algorithm is I/O optimal, because it accesses the minimum number of R–tree nodes required to guarantee that the k nearest neighbor set retrieved is correct.

A significant number of spatial join techniques were proposed in the literature. They can be classified according to whether they operate on indexed data or not. Thus, there are methods that join indexed data, methods that index non-indexed inputs, and approaches that use a single index only. Spatial join methods first pre-process the non-indexed data sets by spatial hashing or sorting and then join pairs of partitions from them that fit in memory. Therefore, methods that directly apply on indexes are usually faster than those that do not rely on indexes because they avoid any pre-processing costs. Besides the filter step of spatial joins, the refinement step has also received attention, due to the increased complexity of verifying a large number of candidate object pairs, whose MBRs intersect.

In order to integrate methods for the evaluation of spatial operations in a DBMS, effective selectivity and cost models for these operations should be defined. The selectivity models depend on the underlying data distribution. For uniform data, it is relatively easy to predict the output size of spatial operations. For non-uniform data, the spatial domain is partitioned into buckets according to the data distribution, such that the locations and sizes of objects in each bucket are as uniform as possible. Uniformity is then assumed within each bucket in order to apply the selectivity models. Cost models for spatial operations are usually derived from selectivity models, because page accesses and R–tree node accesses depend on the data distribution and the location of the query; the cost of spatial operations is usually output sensitive.

BIBLIOGRAPHIC NOTES

Nearest neighbor queries using R–trees have been studied by Roussopoulos et al. [1995] (depth-first search algorithm) and Hjaltason and Samet [1999] (best-first search, incremental NN retrieval). The spatial join algorithm that synchronously traverses R–trees was proposed by Brinkhoff et al. [1993]. Spatial join processing, based on space filling curves was studied by Orenstein and Manola [1988]. A method that transforms spatial data to high dimensional vectors and then indexes them with grid files is proposed by Becker et al. [1993]. Rotem [1991] shows how relational join indexes can be extended to spatial join indices.

Algorithms that do not consider indexes for spatial join evaluation were proposed by Lo and Ravishankar [1996] (spatial hash join), Patel and DeWitt [1996] (partition based spatial merge join), Koudas and Sevcik [1997] (size separation spatial join), and Arge et al. [1998] (scalable sweeping-based spatial join). Single-index based join methods were proposed by Lo and Ravishankar [1994] (seeded tree join), Papadopoulos et al. [1999] (build and match, sort and match), and Mamoulis and Papadias [2003] (slot index spatial join). Mamoulis and Papadias [2001a] extend the binary R–tree join algorithm of Brinkhoff et al. [1993] for multiple inputs and study the optimization (i.e., join ordering) problem for multiway spatial joins. The unified approach for spatial joins is by Arge et al. [2000]. Jacox and Samet [2007] survey and classify spatial join algorithms.

Multi-step spatial query processing using MBRs and other object approximations (conservative and progressive) has been studied by Brinkhoff et al. [1993] (for spatial selections) and Brinkhoff et al. [1994] (for spatial joins). The signature-based method that accelerates the refinement step of spatial joins is proposed by Zimbrao and de Souza [1998]. Distance join evaluation in multi-dimensional spaces is studied by Koudas and Sevcik [2000] and Böhm et al. [2001]. Algorithms for evaluating closest-pairs queries were proposed by Hjaltason and Samet [1998] , Corral et al. [2000], and Shin et al. [2000]. Iceberg distance joins were studied by Shou et al. [2003]. (Figure 4.20 is taken from this paper.)

Muthukrishnan et al. [1999] show that the construction of optimal multi-dimensional histograms is NP-hard. Acharya et al. [1999] propose the min-skew spatial histogram. Another spatial histogram that captures the complexity and size of the spatial objects as well as their location is proposed by Aboulnaga and Naughton [2000]. Spatial histograms for selection queries with arbitrary spatial relationships (besides intersection) are proposed by Sun et al. [2002a] and by Lin et al. [2006]. An accurate approach for estimating the index traversal cost and selectivity of spatial selections, based on an auxiliary data structure, which captures spatial density, is proposed by An et al. [2003].

Estimating the number of R−tree nodes that are accessed during the evaluation of a spatial selection is studied by Theodoridis and Sellis [1996]. This model was then extended to predict the cost and selectivity of spatial joins [Theodoridis et al., 1998]. Selectivity estimation for spatial queries can also be performed efficiently, by analyzing fractal-based data correlations and power-laws for object distances [Belussi and Faloutsos, 1995, Faloutsos et al., 2000]. Tao et al. [2004b] developed the cost model for k-nearest neighbor queries. (Figures 4.2 and 4.4 are taken and modified from this paper.) Selectivity estimation methods for spatial joins with geometric selections were proposed by Mamoulis and Papadias [2001b] and Sun et al. [2002b]. Mamoulis et al. [2005] present an overview of algorithms, cost models and optimization techniques for spatial joins. (Figures 4.7 and 4.15 are taken from this work.)

CHAPTER 5

Spatial Networks

In many real applications the accessibility of objects is restricted by a spatial network. On urban maps, for example, the movement of subjects (e.g., people, cars, etc.) is not free and can only be along road segments. This restriction affects the concepts of proximity and distance. For example, when a car driver is looking for the nearest gas station to fill up her tank, he/she does not necessarily request for the nearest station in terms of geometric (i.e., Euclidean) distance, but for the station, which has the minimum *driving distance* to his/her current position.

To illustrate this issue, consider a user modeled by point q in Figure 5.1, who wants to dine in the nearest restaurant (restaurants are modeled by points r_1, r_2, and r_3 in Figure 5.1). The line segments on the figure correspond to road segments that the user is allowed to walk (or drive) along; movement outside these segments is not possible. Although r_2 is the nearest restaurant in terms of Euclidean distance, it turns out to be the farthest one in terms of road network distance.

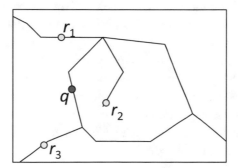

Figure 5.1: Objects on a spatial network.

The road network distance between two points a and b on a spatial network is measured by the *shortest path distance* between a and b. The shortest path between a and b is the path among all those that connect the two points, which has the minimum accumulated length (that is, the minimum sum of lengths of the line segments that the path includes). Computing shortest path distance requires information about the structure of the underlying network. Common spatial query operations, like nearest neighbor search, rely on distance computations. As a result, the management of spatial data over spatial networks requires special treatment. Indexing methods and query evaluation techniques based on Euclidean distance are no longer directly applicable. For example, the R–tree may no longer be appropriate for indexing spatial networks, because it does not capture connectivity information.

Therefore, there is a need of access methods that manage spatial and connectivity information and special evaluation techniques for data that lie on spatial networks.

In this chapter, we present the extensions that are applied on a spatial database system in order to manage spatial networks and data on them. First, we discuss how spatial networks are modeled and how distances between locations in them can be computed. Second, indexing approaches for spatial network data are presented and methods for evaluating common spatial query types for spatial network data are reviewed. Finally, a number of shortest path and network distance materialization approaches, which facilitate efficient shortest path computation are discussed.

5.1   MODELING SPATIAL NETWORKS

A spatial network is a graph, where nodes correspond to connection (i.e., junction) points between continuous segments. The segments (edges) that connect two nodes have simple geometry; typically, they are simplified to straight or curved line segments. The edge connecting two nodes a and b could be directed (e.g., from a to b) or bidirectional. It is possible that multiple edges connect the same pair of nodes. In addition, an edge can be associated with a *weight* modeling the cost of traveling along that edge (e.g., traveling time, fuel cost). In simple networks, an edge weight corresponds to the spatial distance between the connected nodes, i.e., the length of the corresponding line segment.

A straightforward way to model a graph with n nodes is to define an $n \times n$ *adjacency matrix* M, where each element M_{ij} stores information about the edge(s) connecting nodes i and j. Figure 5.2a shows an example of a simple directed graph, which includes 6 nodes, there is only at most one edge per direction for each pair of nodes, and the edges are labeled by weights. The adjacency matrix of Figure 5.2b can model this graph. Each element of the matrix stores the weight of the corresponding edge or '∞' if the edge does not exist. Note that if the graph was bidirectional, the adjacency matrix would be symmetric, since an edge connecting a and b would imply two directed edges $a \rightarrow b$ and $b \rightarrow a$ of the same weight.

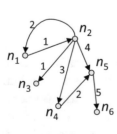

	n_1	n_2	n_3	n_4	n_5	n_6
n_1	0	1	∞	∞	∞	∞
n_2	2	0	1	3	4	∞
n_3	∞	∞	0	∞	∞	∞
n_4	∞	∞	∞	0	2	∞
n_5	∞	∞	∞	∞	0	5
n_6	∞	∞	∞	∞	∞	0

n_1	$(n_2, 1)$
n_2	$(n_1, 2), (n_3, 1), (n_4, 3), (n_5, 4)$
n_4	$(n_5, 2)$
n_5	$(n_6, 5)$

(a) directed graph   (b) adjacency matrix   (c) adjacency lists

Figure 5.2: Examples of simple graph models.

Unlike general graphs (e.g., the Web or social network graphs), spatial networks are very *sparse* by nature. Like the graph shown in Figure 5.2a, the (outgoing or incoming) degree of each node is expected to be small; typically, in road networks, or other spatial networks (e.g., hydrology networks), a small number of segments are connected at a junction. This means that the majority of entries in the adjacency matrix of a spatial network would contain no information (e.g., note that the number of '∞' entries in Figure 5.2b is large) and a lot of space is wasted in such a representation. A more appropriate data model for sparse graphs uses adjacency lists to store the connectivity information. As Figure 5.2b illustrates, for each node n_i in the graph, we can store a list of nodes adjacent to n_i together with the weights of the corresponding edges (e.g., $(n_3, 1)$ in the list of n_2 denotes that there is an edge from n_2 to n_3 with weight 1). The advantage is that we do not have to store any information for pairs of nodes that are not directly connected. A minor drawback is that we now have to perform binary search in the list of n_i if we want to retrieve an edge (n_i, n_j); however, since the lists are expected to be small in sparse graphs, this is not expected to be a significant overhead.

Another characteristic of spatial networks is that they carry spatial information. Nodes correspond to spatial locations and edges also have spatial features. Therefore, the adjacency lists representation alone is not adequate for the efficient support of spatial queries. In addition, if the spatial network graph is too large to fit in memory, we have to manage its representation on disk. In the next section, we discuss how large spatial graphs can be indexed.

5.2   DISK-BASED INDEXING APPROACHES

Connectivity-Clustered Access Method (CCAM) is a secondary memory data structure for very large graphs, which clusters the adjacency lists of nodes into pages based on their connectivity. The goal of the index is to guide graph traversal, while minimizing the I/O. CCAM first indexes the nodes of the graph with a B^+-tree, using their identifiers as key. The identifiers of nodes are given according to their order on a Z-curve (refer to Section 3.1.2 for details on ordering spatial data using space filling curves), in order to facilitate spatial searching for graph nodes. Each leaf node entry of the B^+-tree, corresponding to a graph node n_i, is linked to the disk page, which stores the adjacency list of n_i. The adjacency lists of nodes are packed into disk pages, according to a connectivity optimization criterion, which minimizes the ratio of edges stored in the adjacency lists that lead to nodes outside the page. In other words, the adjacency lists of connected nodes are stored in the same disk page with high probability. Figure 5.3a illustrates an exemplary spatial graph and Figure 5.3b shows the corresponding CCAM index. Note that the graph is partitioned into two subgraphs, each corresponding to a disk page of adjacency lists. For example, the adjacency lists of n_1, n_3, n_5 are stored in page p_1. The B^+-tree is used to locate fast the adjacency list of a given node (e.g., n_1). Traversing the graph from n_1 to a neighbor node n_3 does not to incur an I/O, since the adjacency lists of n_1 and n_3 are stored in the same disk page (p_1).

The basic version of CCAM does not index the spatial information of graph edges; therefore, spatial queries that refer to information on graph edges (i.e., objects or spatial locations that may lie on edges, not necessarily on graph nodes) may not be efficiently evaluated. An extension of this

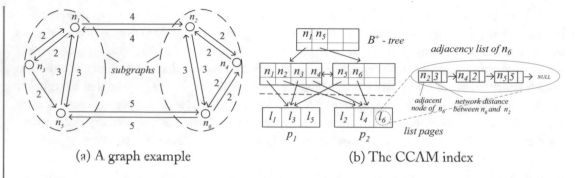

(a) A graph example (b) The CCAM index

Figure 5.3: Example of CCAM.

data structure indexes the spatial extent of edges, in order to facilitate spatial search, while retaining the connectivity-based indexing module of the basic CCAM index. The extended CCAM index consists of three components. The *adjacency component*, as in the basic CCAM, captures the network connectivity. The *polyline component*, stores the detailed geometric (i.e., polyline) representation of each edge in the network. There is also a *network R–tree* that indexes the MBRs of the polylines (i.e., edges) and supports queries exploring the spatial properties of the network. Figure 5.4 illustrates this indexing architecture.

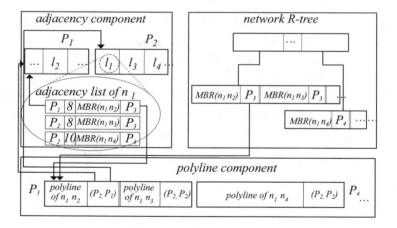

Figure 5.4: An extended version of CCAM.

In the adjacency component, the adjacency lists of the nodes close in the network are placed in the same disk page. Consider the adjacency list l_1 of node n_1. Each entry in this list corresponds to a graph edge (e.g., (n_1, n_2)) and stores the disk page (e.g., P_1) which stores the adjacency list of the corresponding destination node (e.g., n_2), the weight of the edge (e.g., 8), the minimum bounding rectangle (MBR) of the edge's geometry (i.e., a polyline), and a pointer to the disk page in the polyline component which stores the polyline (e.g., P_3). Each entry in a page of the polyline component stores the exact geometry of an edge (n_i, n_j) together with the a pair of pointers to the disk pages containing the adjacency lists of its endpoints n_i and n_j. Finally, each leaf node entry of the network R–tree stores the MBR of a polyline and a pointer to the page in the polyline component that contains the exact geometric representation of the edge.

The index supports spatial search operations, such as finding the edge of the network that contains a query point q. For example, consider a car driver, who wants to find the road segment, where he is currently located, on a digital transportation map. If the map is indexed by the access method described above, we can use the network R–tree to find MBRs that contain the query point and then the polyline component to refine the search. If the point is not found to lie on an edge, the nearest edge can be used to *snap* the point on it. For example, it is possible that due to GPS reception errors the location of a driver is shown to be outside the transportation network. In this case, the nearest road segment is expected to be the most accurate.

The index also supports network traversal operations. For example, assume that we want to retrieve the edges that are within a given traveling distance from our current location. First, we can use the network R–tree component to find the edge that contains our current location, as explained in the previous paragraph. Then, we can apply a traversal on the graph with the help of the adjacency component to access the neighboring edges and repeat this process by accessing neighboring edges that have not been seen before, while their accumulated distances do not exceed the threshold. In the next section, we discuss in detail methods that traverse the graph in order to compute shortest path distances.

5.3   SHORTEST PATH COMPUTATION

Shortest path search is a core component of distance-based queries in graphs. The problem of finding the shortest path from a source node s to a destination node t in a graph is a classic one with a large number of approaches proposed in the literature. In this section, we review some of them.

5.3.1   DIJKSTRA'S ALGORITHM

Dijkstra's algorithm, described by the pseudocode of Figure 5.5, is a popular method for computing the shortest path from a source node s to a destination node t in a graph. Starting from s, the algorithm traverses the graph, prioritizing visits to nodes that are closer to s, until t is found during the graph browsing.

In particular, the algorithm first initializes the shortest paths and distances from s to all nodes in the graph to null and infinity, respectively. It marks all nodes as unvisited. The shortest path distance from s to itself is set to 0 and s is added to a priority queue Q, which organizes the graph nodes v added to it, according to their shortest path distances $SPD(s, v)$ from s. While the heap Q is not empty, the node v with the smallest $SPD(s, v)$ is de-heaped. When this happens, the shortest path from s to v is guaranteed to be found and the currently recorded shortest path distance

function $Dijkstra\_SP$(source node s, target node t)
1.   **for each** graph node v
2. $SPD(s, v) := \infty;$ /* initialize shortest path distance */
3. $path(s, v) := null;$ /* initialize shortest path */
4.   mark v as unvisited;
5.   initialize a priority queue Q;
6. $SPD(s, s) := 0;$ add s to Q;
7.   **while** not $empty(Q)$
8. $v := top(Q);$ /* node v on Q with smallest $SPD(s, v)$ */
9.   remove v from Q;
10.   mark v as visited;
11.   **if** $v = t$ then return $path(s, t)$;
12.   **for each** neighbor u of v
13.   **if** u is not marked as visited
14.   **if** $SPD(s, u) > SPD(s, v) + weight(v, u)$
15. $SPD(s, u) := SPD(s, v) + weight(v, u)$;
16. $path(s, u) := path(s, v) + (v, u)$;
17.   add or update u on Q;

Figure 5.5: Dijkstra's shortest path computation algorithm.

$SPD(s, v)$ is guaranteed to be correct; v is marked as visited and the algorithm will not consider it again. If v happens to be the target node t, the algorithm terminates reporting $path(s, t)$. Otherwise, the neighbors of v are examined. For each neighbor u, we check whether its current shortest path from s can be updated, i.e., whether the path to u that passes through v is shorter than any path to u previously found. We update u's path and distance, accordingly, and add u on Q (if not already there) or update it according to the changed $SPD(s, v)$ value. Note that $w(v, u)$ denotes the weight of edge (v, u); if multiple directed edges exist from v to u, the one with the minimum weight is used. The computational cost of the algorithm for spatial networks (i.e., sparse graphs) is bounded by $O(m + n \log n)$, where m and n are the number of edges and nodes, respectively.

As an example, consider the graph of Figure 5.2a and assume that we want to compute the shortest path between $s = n_2$ and $t = n_6$. First, we add n_2 on Q and initialize the shortest path distances (SPDs) of all other nodes to infinity. The first node to be de-heaped is n_2. Since n_2 is not the target node, we examine its neighbors n_4 and n_5 and because their current SPDs are infinite, we update them to $SPD(n_2, n_4) = SPD(n_2, n_2) + weight(n_2, n_4) = 0 + 3 = 3$ and $SPD(n_2, n_5) = 4$, and set the corresponding current shortest paths to $path(n_2, n_4) = (n_2, n_4)$ and $path(n_2, n_5) = (n_2, n_5)$. Nodes n_4 and n_5 are added on Q. The next node to be de-heaped is n_4, because it has the currently minimum SPD. The neighbors of n_4 are examined; the only neighbor of n_4 is n_5, which is already on the heap. We examine whether the current $SPD(n_2, n_5)$ is larger than $SPD(n_2, n_4) + weight(n_4, n_5)$. The answer is negative, so there is no update of $SPD(n_2, n_5)$ and $path(n_2, n_5)$. The next node to be de-heaped is n_5. Its only neighbor is n_6, which is en-heaped after setting $SPD(n_2, n_6) = SPD(n_2, n_5) + weight(n_5, n_6) = 9$ and $path(n_2, n_6) = path(n_2, n_5) + (n_5, n_6)$. In the next loop, the target node n_6 is removed from Q, and the shortest path $n_2 \rightarrow n_5 \rightarrow n_6$ is output as the result of the search process.

5.3.2 A^* SEARCH

In spatial networks, the Euclidean distance can be used to lower-bound the shortest path distance between any pair of nodes. Assume that the weight of any edge in a spatial network is equal to the geometric distance between the corresponding pair of nodes. Then, obviously the shortest path distance is always larger than or equal to the Euclidean distance between the corresponding pair of nodes. For example, in the network of Figure 5.1, the shortest path network distance between points q and r_1 is larger than their Euclidean distance. This Euclidean-based bound of the shortest path can be used by a variant of Dijkstra's algorithm, called the A^*-algorithm, to accelerate shortest path search. The change to be made in the algorithm is very simple; instead of prioritizing the access order of the nodes in Q, according to their current SPD from the source, we prioritize them by their current SPD increased by the lower bound of their Euclidean distance to the target node. Thus, for a node v, its key in the priority Q is now $SPD(s,v) + dist(v,t)$, where $dist(v,t)$ is the Euclidean distance between v and t. This heuristic order gives higher access priority to nodes that are geometrically closer to the target node t and avoids accessing parts of the graph that are geometrically far from the target. By altering the access order in this way, the correctness of the algorithm is not affected, since when t is de-heaped, its exact $SPD(s,t)$ would have been computed and it would be the lowest SPD among all nodes currently on the heap Q.

To illustrate the functionality of the A^*-algorithm, consider the spatial network of Figure 5.6a. Note that the edge weights are the distances between the corresponding nodes and the graph is undirected (i.e., the directed edge weights are symmetric). Assume that we have to compute the shortest path between nodes s and t. Like in Dijkstra, s is the first node to be added to the queue Q. When s is de-heaped, its neighbors a, c, and d are examined and added to the heap. For each neighbor v, together with $SPD(s,v)$, we compute the bound $SPD(s,v) + dist(v,t)$ and use it as the lower bound for the shortest path distance $SPD(s,t)$. This quantity is used to order the nodes in the heap. The next node to be de-queued is c, because $SPD(s,c) + dist(c,t)$ is smaller than $SPD(s,a) + dist(a,t)$ and $SPD(s,d) + dist(d,t)$. Note that $SPD(s,c)$ is larger than $SPD(s,d)$ and $SPD(s,a)$, and that d would be visited next by Diijkstra's algorithm instead of c. Therefore, A^* follows a different order than Diijkstra's algorithm, favoring visits to nodes that are closer to the target in terms of Euclidean distance and reaching the target faster. In this example, A^* finds the shortest path $s \rightarrow c \rightarrow e \rightarrow t$ by visiting only nodes c, e and t, while Diijkstra's algorithm would have to visit all nodes in the graph before t, in order to terminate (observe that all nodes have smaller SPD from s than t).

5.3.3   BI-DIRECTIONAL SEARCH

Dijkstra's algorithm expands the network around the source node s, computing s's shortest paths to other nodes incrementally, until the target node t is found. The shortest path can also be found by the same algorithm symmetrically, by computing all shortest paths that have t as destination, incrementally until the source node s is found. For this, the algorithm starts from t and considers the inverted edges for the backward network expansion.

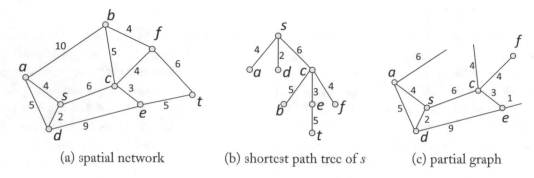

(a) spatial network   (b) shortest path tree of s (c) partial graph

Figure 5.6: A shortest path tree on a spatial network.

The expected cost of such a backward search is similar to that of forward search. However, it is possible to reduce the search cost if we initiate one forward (i.e., from s) and one backward (i.e., from t) search concurrently. The *bi-directional* search algorithm is based on this idea. The algorithm incrementally computes (i) the shortest paths from s to all other nodes and (ii) the shortest paths to t from all other nodes. Two Dijkstra searches are run concurrently with the help of two heaps Q_s and Q_t, for the forward and backward search, respectively.

At each step, the node v with the smallest $r_{s,t}(v) = \min\{SPD(s, v), SPD(v, t)\}$ is visited; i.e., from the top elements of the two priority queues Q_s and Q_t, the one with the smallest distance. If, for a visited node v from forward search, v appears in the queue Q_t, then a candidate shortest path P has been found. Path P consists of three parts: (i) $path(s, v)$ (found by forward search), (ii) edge (v, u), where u is the node that has been visited by backward search and is the node responsible for v's value on Q_t, and (iii) $path(u, t)$, which is the shortest path from visited node u (by backward search) to t. A candidate shortest path can also be found symmetrically whenever a node is visited by backward search and also appears in Q_s. Bi-directional search keeps track of the best candidate shortest path found so far during search. Search terminates as soon as a node v is visited by forward search and has already visited by backward search in the past (or vice versa).

As an example, assume that we want to find the shortest path from s to t in the graph of Figure 5.6a using bi-directional search. We initiate two concurrent searches, by adding to Q_s nodes d, a, c and to Q_t nodes e, f. From all these nodes the one with the minimum forward or backward distance is d (i.e., the top element of Q_s with distance 2 from s). Therefore, the algorithm visits d and adds to Q_s node e. The next node to be visited is a (again from Q_s), which en-heaps node b to Q_s. Next, node e is visited, this time from Q_t, which en-heaps nodes c and d to Q_t. Because e appears on Q_s, we have the first candidate shortest path $path(s, d) + (d, e) + path(e, t)$ with total distance 16. The next node to be visited is node c from s. Note that c appears on Q_t; therefore, we have another candidate shortest path $path(s, c) + (c, e) + path(e, t)$, with cost 14, which becomes the currently optimal path. Next, the algorithm visits f from t and adds b to Q_t. Finally, c is visited from t, which has already been visited from s. Therefore, the termination condition has been reached and the path $s \rightarrow c \rightarrow e \rightarrow t$ (i.e., the best candidate) is reported.

5.3.4 SPEEDING-UP SEARCH BY PREPROCESSING

Bi-directional shortest path search can be sped-up with the help of some preprocessing. The idea is based on a *reach* quantity that has to be pre-computed for every node v of the network. Let s, t, be a source-target node pair that passes through v. The *local reach* of v, with respect to s, t, is defined by $r_{s,t}(v) = \min\{SPD(s, v), SPD(v, t)\}$, i.e., v's minimum distance to any of the source/destination nodes. The *global reach* $r(v)$ of v is then the *maximum* of all local reaches for all pairs of nodes s, t, such that the shortest path from s to t passes through v. Therefore, $r(v)$ tells us in the worst case, what is the minimum distance from v to any of s, t, given that v is in the shortest path from s to t.

Now consider again the bi-directional search algorithm. Assume that a node v is visited by forward search (the case of backward search is symmetric). Note that after v's visit, (i) $SPD(s, v)$ has been finalized and (ii) for any *unvisited* node u (either by forward or backward search) $SPD(s, v) \leq SPD(s, u)$ and $SPD(s, v) \leq SPD(u, t)$. Therefore, if $r(u) < SPD(s, v)$, then $r(u) < SPD(s, u)$ and $r(u) < SPD(u, t)$; i.e., if $r(u) < SPD(s, v)$ and due to the definition of $r(u)$, u *cannot be in the shortest path from s to t*. As a result, whenever a node v is visited, its unvisited neighbors u, for which $r(u) < SPD(s, v)$, can be pruned and need not be en-heaped. This reach-based pruning heuristic reduces the search space drastically and makes bi-directional search very fast.

For example, consider the graph of Figure 5.6a and all shortest paths that include b. The maximum local reach of all these paths is due to path $a \rightarrow b \rightarrow f$, i.e., $r(b) = 4$. Therefore, during the computation of the shortest path from s to t, b never has to be considered as soon as node e is visited from t, because b is not visited by that time and $r(b) < SPD(e, t)$.

Precomputing the reach values of all nodes can be expensive, since it involves finding all shortest paths. In addition, updating these values can be expensive after changes in the graph, because all affected shortest paths and related nodes in them should be considered. Therefore, this heuristic is mostly appropriate for static graphs, where pre-computation is only done once and used for any shortest path search thereafter.

5.3.5 QUERY POINTS ON GRAPH EDGES

So far, we have assumed that the points between which we want to compute the shortest path are nodes of the network. In spatial applications, however, the query points could reside anywhere on the graph. For example, when a driver requests the shortest path from her current position to a point of interest on a transportation map (e.g., a gas station), the source and target points of the path query are not necessarily at junctions of the network and they may be on any location on the network edges. Diijkstra's algorithm (and its variants) can straightforwardly be applied in this case. We introduce two additional artificial nodes in the network, one for the source and one for the destination points (if they lie on edges but not on nodes). For each of the new nodes, the neighbors are the end-points of the edge where the source (or target) point lies. This means that the end-points of the edge where the source node lies are the first to be added on the heap together with their corresponding path distances (and bounds). The data structure or index for the network is not altered, since the artificial nodes are not permanently added to the network; when an end-point v of the edge that contains the target node is visited, the target is considered in v's neighborhood together with v's real network neighbors. As a final note, Dijkstra's algorithm (and its variants) are appropriate only for graphs with non-negative edges, like the case of spatial networks. In general graphs, where there may be negative edges other techniques (like the Bellman-Ford algorithm) are applicable.

5.4 EVALUATION OF SPATIAL QUERIES OVER SPATIAL NETWORKS

Spatial queries that do not consider network distances are not affected by whether the spatial data lie on a spatial network. For example, a spatial selection, which requests for the spatial data (or the part of the network) that lie inside a user-defined window, can be processed with the help of a classic spatial index (e.g., an R–tree that indexes the spatial data or the network edges). On the other hand, queries that consider the connectivity or distance information from the network, require special evaluation techniques.

5.4.1 DISTANCE-BASED SPATIAL SELECTION

A distance-based spatial selection requests the set of objects in a spatial relation R that are not further than a network distance bound ϵ to a reference object q. Consider, for example, the following distance-based spatial selection query: "find all gas stations within 5km driving distance from my current location". This query retrieves all spatial objects (i.e., gas stations) that appear on any node or edge of the spatial network at most ϵ=5km from a reference location q. The spatial network and the spatial data are usually stored at different layers: one layer for the network (indexed using some of the methods discussed in Section 5.2) and one layer (i.e., spatial relation) for the spatial data. Therefore, to evaluate the query an intuitive strategy is to first retrieve the part of the network that qualifies the distance constraint and then use the result as a classic spatial selection query on the (indexed) spatial data (e.g., gas stations) to retrieve the results.

Note that, although in Section 5.3, we introduced Dijkstra's algorithm as a method for shortest path search from a source node s to a target t, the algorithm can directly be applied to generate the *shortest path tree* of s, i.e., a tree that includes the shortest paths from s to all other nodes. For example, the shortest path tree of node s in Figure 5.6a is shown in Figure 5.6b. In other words, Dijkstra's algorithm, *incrementally* computes the distance (and the respective path) from s to any other node. As soon as one node v is visited by the algorithm (i.e., de-heaped from Q), v is added to the tree together with its corresponding shortest path. In fact, only the last edge of the path is used to connect v as a child of its predecessor in the shortest path.

If we compute the shortest path tree for only those nodes up to the distance constraint ϵ and add to it all other seen edges and parts thereof that qualify the distance constraint (these are all reachable from the shortest path tree nodes), then we can form the region of a spatial selection query. For example, Figure 5.6c shows the area of the network in Figure 5.6a which contains all locations at most distance $\epsilon=10$ from s. This query is applied against the R–tree that indexes the spatial relation R to retrieve the results of the spatial selection.

Another approach for answering the distance based spatial selection query is to take advantage of a Euclidean distance bound to prune the search space. Consider a spatial network (e.g., a road network) and assume that the objects of the spatial relation R are sparsely distributed in the network (i.e., the majority of network edges do not have any objects on them). In this case, we can first run a simple spatial selection query against the R–tree that indexes R and retrieve the set of objects that are within Euclidean distance ϵ from q. Any object that is not retrieved by this query cannot be part of the network distance query, because the network distance is lower-bounded by the Euclidean distance. Therefore, the objects that we retrieve are candidate results for the network distance query. For each such candidate, we run a shortest-path query (e.g., using A^*) to verify their actual SPD to q and report them as answers if the distance does not exceed ϵ.

5.4.2 NEAREST-NEIGHBOR RETRIEVAL

Nearest neighbor retrieval is not very different compared to distance based selection. Again, there is a reference point q, but this time there is no fixed distance constraint; instead, we want to retrieve from relation R the k nearest objects to location q. For example, q could be the location of a user in a city and R could store the locations of restaurants. The user is interested in the k nearest restaurants to his location in terms of network distance.

Like in the distance query case, we can use Dijkstra's algorithm to browse the network nodes in increasing distance from q. Whenever we find an edge, for which the shortest path distance to q has been determined (this happens when we know the SPD of the edge end-points), we use the edge as a spatial selection query against the R–tree of R and compute the shortest path distances of all objects on that edge to q. The k-th nearest neighbor network distance found so far can be used as a termination bound for Dijkstra's browsing algorithm. That is, as soon there is a guarantee that for the unvisited nodes and their connecting edges, the network distance of any objects on them is no smaller than the k-th nearest neighbor distance, we stop visiting any more nodes and report the query results.

An alternative to browsing network nodes and edges incrementally and searching for objects on them is to use the Euclidean nearest neighbors to guide search. To comprehend this *Incremental Euclidean Restriction* (IER) approach, consider the example illustrated in Figure 5.7. Assume that we are interested in the nearest neighbor of q in the network space. First, we use the R–tree that indexes R to find the Euclidean nearest neighbor of q. That is point p_{E1}, which becomes the candidate nearest neighbor of q. We then apply a shortest path search (e.g., using A^*) to retrieve the network distance $d_N(q, p_{E1})$ from q to p_{E1} and the corresponding path (see Figure 5.7a). Due to the bounding property of the Euclidean distance, any point with Euclidean distance greater than $d_N(q, p_{E1})$ cannot be closer to q than p_{E1}, in terms of network distance. Therefore, only points in the shaded ring of Figure 5.7a can potentially be closer to q than p_{E1} is. We continue the incremental Euclidean NN search and retrieve the next neighbor p_{E2} (see Figure 5.7b). This point is within the ring and $d_N(q, p_{E2}) < d_N(q, p_{E1})$; therefore, p_{E2} becomes the new network NN candidate and the ring area that may contain better candidates is shrunk (its outer radius is now $d_N(q, p_{E2})$). Observe that the next Euclidean neighbor (p_{E3}) is outside the ring; therefore, search can now be terminated and p_{E2} is guaranteed to be the network-based nearest neighbor of q.

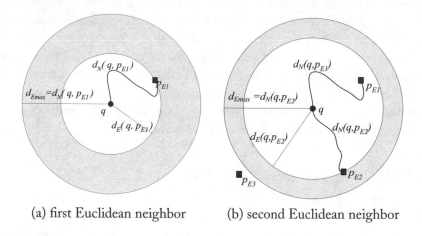

(a) first Euclidean neighbor   (b) second Euclidean neighbor

Figure 5.7: Incremental Euclidean Restriction for nearest neighbor search.

5.4.3   JOIN QUERIES

Join queries can also be expressed for pairs of spatial relations, using the network distance of objects in the join predicate. For example, we may be interested in all pairs of restaurants and hotels with shortest path distance at most ϵ. The techniques that we have discussed so far can be easily adapted to process join queries. For example, a possible evaluation strategy is to run, for each restaurant location, a network distance based spatial selection using threshold ϵ, to retrieve all hotels in the restaurant's vicinity. Another evaluation strategy would be to first run a Euclidean ϵ-distance join method to find all pairs of restaurants and hotels within Euclidean distance ϵ from each other. Each of these pairs becomes a candidate for the respective network distance join query and a shortest path query is run to verify whether the pair's network distance indeed does not exceed ϵ.

5.5   PATH MATERIALIZATION TECHNIQUES

Shortest path computations dominate the cost of spatial queries over networks. Therefore, there have been many efforts for reducing this cost with the help of path materialization and advanced indexing approaches. An aggressive way to reduce the cost of shortest path search is to materialize the shortest paths (and the respective distances) for every pair of nodes in the network. By doing so, the cost of shortest path search is reduced to $O(1)$. Figure 5.8a shows (partially) the shortest path materialization matrix for every source-destination pair of nodes from the graph of Figure 5.7a. To retrieve the shortest path between a pair of nodes (e.g., from a to c), we just have to access the corresponding cell in the matrix (e.g., cell in row a and column c gives path $a \rightarrow s \rightarrow c$ having distance 10). However, the space requirements of such a method can be as high as $O(n^3)$, for a network of n nodes, since there are $O(n^2)$ pairs and the length of a path can be $O(n)$.

	a	b	c	s	...
a	0,-	10, ab	10, asc	4, as	...
b	10, ba	0,-	5, bc	11, bcs	...
c	10, csa	5,cb	0,-	6,cs	...
s	4, sa	11, scb	6, sc	0,-	...
...	...	...	...	...	...

	a	b	c	s	...
a	0, -	10, b	10, s	4, s	...
b	10, a	0, -	5, c	11, c	...
c	10, s	5, b	0, -	6, s	...
s	4, a	11, c	6, c	0, -	...
...	...	...	...	...	...

(a) brute-force materialization   (b) distance matrix with path successors

Figure 5.8: Shortest path materialization approaches.

A less aggressive approach stores only the shortest path distances between every pair of nodes in a $n \times n$ matrix. In some search operations, only the distance (not the path) is required for a pair of graph nodes (for example when comparing network distances with Euclidean distance bounds in nearest neighbor retrieval). The matrix can directly be used to find the distance between any pair in $O(1)$ time; however, finding shortest paths still requires graph traversal. For simple spatial networks, which we have seen so far, a *subpath optimality* property facilitates encoding the paths in the distance matrix as well, without increasing the space complexity. Consider the shortest path $SP(s, t) = s \rightarrow \cdots \rightarrow v \rightarrow \cdots \rightarrow t$ from s to t, which passes through v; subpath optimality ensures that the shortest path from v to t is identical to the sub-path $v \rightarrow \cdots \rightarrow t$ included in $SP(s, t)$. Therefore, if, in the shortest path distance matrix, together with the shortest distance $SPD(u, v)$ between every pair of nodes u, v, we store the successor node $succ(u)$ of u in the shortest path $SP(u, v)$, we can retrieve $SP(u, v)$, by visiting cell $(succ(u), v)$, then cell $(succ(succ(u)), v)$, etc. This partial materialization approach is illustrated in Figure 5.8b (for the data of Figure 5.7a). For example, to retrieve the shortest path from a to c, we first access cell (a, c), which gives us edge $a \rightarrow s$ and then cell (s, c), which gives us edge $s \rightarrow c$. Therefore, the retrieval of a shortest path of length l requires $O(l)$ accesses to the matrix.

Still, the $O(n^2)$ space requirements and the additional $O(n)$ worst-case cost for retrieving the shortest path of a given pair of nodes could be too high in practice. Apart from these issues, path materialization also has a high maintenance cost, if network nodes and edge weights are subject to updates. In the following, we discuss some more sophisticated indexing approaches which have been proposed to facilitate shortest path search.

5.5.1   HIERARCHICAL PATH MATERIALIZATION

In order to reduce the space demands of path materialization, a divide-and-conquer approach can be applied to hierarchically partition the graph into multiple levels. Initially, the original graph is divided into a set of regions based on the connectivity and proximity of nodes. The partitioning is done such that every edge of the graph is assigned to exactly one partition. However, there can be *border* nodes, which belong to more than one partitions (for example, if edge (v, u) falls in one partition and edge (u, w) in another, then u becomes a border node). Figure 5.9a illustrates a graph, which is partitioned into three regions as shown in Figure 5.9b. The nodes marked by rectangles are border nodes, and they may be replicated to different partitions.

For each partition, all shortest paths between every pair of nodes are materialized and encoded, with the help of a shortest-path distance matrix. The partitioning ensures that the size of each region is small enough for the matrix to be of manageable size. The border nodes are handled at the upper layer of the data structure. Again a shortest-path distance matrix is generated for the border nodes, considering the whole graph for computing shortest paths. If the number of border nodes is too large and materialization of all shortest paths is not efficient, the border nodes are recursively divided to groups and a higher-level set of border nodes is chosen from them.

In order to evaluate a shortest path query from s to t, we first find the partitions where s and t belong and whether any of them is a border node. Depending on this information, we act as follows:

- If s and t are both border nodes, then the matrix for border nodes is directly used to find the shortest path.

- If s is a border node and t is a non-border node, then the answer is the shortest among all paths $path(s, u) + path(u, t)$, for all border nodes u in the partition P_t of t.

- If s is a non-border node and t is a border node, then the answer is the shortest among all paths $path(s, u) + path(u, t)$, for all border nodes u in the partition P_s of s.

- If both s and t are non-border nodes, then the shortest of the following paths is returned: (i) the shortest path between s and t materialized in the partition P_{st} if s and t belong to the same partition, (ii) the shortest among all paths $path(s, u) + path(u, v) + path(v, t)$, where u and v are border nodes and belong to partitions P_s and P_t, respectively.

For example, consider the problem of computing the shortest path between nodes s and t in Figure 5.9, which belong to partitions P_3 and P_2, respectively. Since the nodes belong to different partitions, their shortest path should go through some border nodes. Therefore the path should be one of the shortest paths that connects s to a border node u of P_3, then connects u to a border node v of P_2 and then connects v to t. For each combination, we can use the materialized information to retrieve the shortest paths for the corresponding connections and concatenate them to a candidate shortest path.

A good hierarchical partitioning approach restricts the number of combinations to be examined; therefore, a good bound for the cost can be derived, while making the partitions small enough in order to have a low computational and storage cost for the matrices that materialize the shortest paths within a partition.

   Real road networks can naturally be partitioned hierarchically by placing non-highway nodes in local regions and setting highway nodes as border nodes. For example, a typical shortest path between two locations in a city involve taking local roads until a highway, then taking a segment of the highway and then another set of local nodes until the destination is reached. By materializing the shortest paths between every pair of highway exits and the shortest paths between nodes in the same neighborhood, shortest path retrieval can become very efficient.

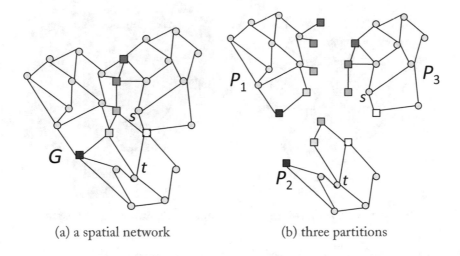

(a) a spatial network   (b) three partitions

Figure 5.9: Hierarchical partitioning of a spatial graph.

5.5.2   COMPRESSING AND INDEXING MATERIALIZED PATHS

As already mentioned, the $O(n^2)$ space requirements of the distance matrix (with path successors) make it impractical for materializing shortest paths in large graphs. The storage cost of the matrix can be reduced for spatial graphs, by taking advantage of the facts that (i) each node s has a low degree and that (ii) the shortest paths from s to nodes that are spatially close, typically share the same successor of s. For example, consider the graph of Figure 5.10a and the shortest paths from s to all other nodes. Each candidate target node t takes the same color as the successor of s in the shortest path from s to t. Observe that the nodes of the same color are spatially clustered.

   The *Spatial Induced Linkage Cognizance* (SILC) framework builds on this observation to materialize and index the shortest paths from any candidate source node s effectively. For each neighbor node v of s, SILC defines a space partition that includes all nodes t for which the shortest path from s to t has v as s's successor. The partitions are disjoint to each other and they are indexed with the help of a spatial access method. For example, in the network of Figure 5.10a, the nodes can be partitioned into four regions, one for each successor of s, as shown in Figure 5.10b. Note that the regions may have irregular shapes. An appropriate access method for indexing them is a quadtree, after decomposing them to maximal quadrants that contain only points of the same color (i.e., the same successor). Therefore, for every node of the network, which can be a candidate source for a shortest path query, a space decomposition is defined for the remaining network nodes. The space requirements for storing and indexing the decomposition are expected to be much lower than $O(n)$ (in typical networks they are $O(n^{1/2})$); therefore, the overall cost of this path materialization approach is $O(n^{3/2})$, which is much lower than the $O(n^2)$ space overhead of the distance matrix.

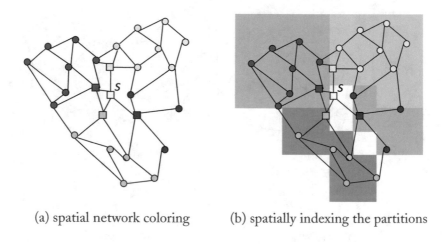

(a) spatial network coloring   (b) spatially indexing the partitions

Figure 5.10: Compressed representations of all shortest paths from node s.

In order to retrieve the shortest path from a source node s to a target node t, we first access the index for s, to find the color of the region where t resides. From this, we identify the successor v of s in the shortest path. Then, we access the index for v, again trying to locate t in it, to get the next successor. The process continues until the entire shortest path is retrieved.

5.5.3   EMBEDDING METHODS

Recall that A^*-search uses the Euclidean distance between two nodes as a lower bound of their network distance. This bound in many cases is very loose and it misleads the search algorithm. For example, in Figure 5.1, the Euclidean distance between q and r_2 is very small compared to the corresponding shortest path distance.

In effect, the Euclidean distance between two network nodes is their distance in an *embedded* space (i.e., the Euclidean cartesian space). In order to derive better bounds for network distance, a number of more sophisticated embedding methods have been developed. The goal of embedding the network nodes to another space is to be able to derive a computationally cheap lower bound of the distance between any pair of nodes, which is as tight as possible.

Typical embeddings are based on a selected subset L of the network nodes, called *landmarks*. For each landmark, all shortest paths distances from/to other nodes are computed and, based on them, a lower bound for the network distance between any pair of nodes is derived. For example, given a shortest path query from s to t, quantity $|SPD(s, v) - SPD(v, t)|$ for any landmark v serves as a lower bound, due to the triangular inequality property satisfied by the shortest path distance metric. The maximum of these landmark-based lower bounds (i.e., $\max_{v \in L}\{|SPD(s, v) - SPD(v, t)|\}$) can be used to replace the Euclidean distance bound during A^*-search.

For example, consider the graph of Figure 5.6a, and assume that nodes c and d are selected as landmarks and their network distances from/to all nodes are precomputed. Then any node of the network can be mapped to a two-dimensional point, based on its distance to the two landmarks c and d. For example, node a is mapped to point $p_a = (10, 5)$. To derive a lower bound for the distance from s to t, we just have to compute the infinity norm distance between points $p_s = (6, 2)$ and $p_t = (8, 14)$ in the embedded space, i.e., $\max\{|6 - 8|, |2 - 14|\} = 12$.

5.6   SUMMARY

Evaluation of queries over spatial networks is challenging due to the involvement of expensive shortest path computations. Shortest path retrieval is a classic subject in computer science. Methods for general graphs include Dijkstra's algorithm and its extensions (A^*-search, bi-directional search, reach-based search).

To store and index spatial data that lie on spatial networks, main-memory graph representations should be extended to disk-based data structures. CCAM and its extensions partition the graph nodes according to their connectivity and spatial proximity and cluster their adjacency lists in disk pages, such that I/O due to graph traversal is minimized.

Spatial queries that are based on distance computation require the computation of shortest paths or shortest path trees, which can be resource-demanding. Euclidean distance is often used as a cheap lower bound for network distance, to minimize graph traversal operations. Embedding methods that precompute the shortest paths between all nodes and a designated subset of nodes can be used to define more accurate bounds.

The special nature of spatial networks (low average degree per node, edge weights correspond to spatial distances, sources/destinations with similar paths are spatially clustered) allow for more efficient shortest path retrieval methods, compared to general graph browsing techniques. These specialized techniques typically rely on the pre-computation and materialization of shortest paths. Exhaustive materialization of the shortest paths between all pairs is prohibitively expensive for large graphs and different approaches have been proposed to reduce this cost. Some of them apply a hierarchical graph decomposition and materialize all paths between nodes in the same partition and all paths between border nodes that connect partitions together. Others partition the destination nodes of all shortest paths from a given source into regions and spatially index the regions. Finally, embedding approaches precompute all shortest path distances from/to a designated subset of 'landmark' nodes and use them to derive tight lower bounds for network distance during search.

BIBLIOGRAPHIC NOTES

The disk-based CCAM indexing approach for large graphs was proposed by Shekhar and Liu [1997] and extended by Papadias et al. [2003] to include the geometry of network edges.

Dijkstra [1959] introduced the classic single source shortest path algorithm, which was followed by the ideas of bidirectional search [Nicholson, 1966] and A^*-search [Hart et al., 1968]. Gutman [2004] introduced the reach preprocessing method for accelerating Dijkstra's algorithm, which was later [Goldberg et al., 2006] improved and used in combination with bidirectional search and landmark-based A^*-search.

The evaluation of distance-based queries for spatial data that lie on spatial networks was studied by Papadias et al. [2003], who introduced the use of Euclidean bounds to prune the search space in distance-based spatial selection and nearest neighbor retrieval. (Figures 5.3, 5.4, and 5.7 are taken from this paper.)

There is a large body of literature on path pre-processing and materialization approaches to speed up shortest path search; an exhaustive coverage is not possible within the scope of this book.

Agrawal and Jagadish [1989] propose a general encoding scheme for path materialization, which subsumes the scheme that stores for each source-destination pair of nodes u, v, their distance $SPD(u, v)$ and the successor node of u in the corresponding shortest path.

The SILC approach, for space-efficient materialization of all shortest paths was introduced by Samet's group [Samet et al., 2008, Sankaranarayanan et al., 2005] on top of which an efficient nearest neighbor search algorithm was proposed.

Several landmark-based bounds have been proposed and used for shortest path search [Agrawal and Jagadish, 1994, Goldberg and Harrelson, 2005] and for spatial queries, like nearest neighbor search, in road networks [Kriegel et al., 2007, Shahabi et al., 2003].

Bast et al. [2007] showed that for large real road networks, there is a subset of *transit* nodes T, such that at least 99% of the shortest paths between any pair of nodes in the graphs (except those pairs of nodes very close to each other) pass through at least one node from T. Therefore, by preprocessing shortest paths from/to transit nodes, shortest path queries can be greatly accelerated. Abraham et al. [2010] formalized this property to a concept of *highway dimension* for graphs, which models the easiness of a graph to be searched by path materialization heuristics.

Hierarchical shortest path materialization approaches have been proposed by Jing et al. [1998] and Jung and Pramanik [2002].

Sankaranarayanan and Samet [2009] observed that for two map regions A and B, which are far from each other, the shortest paths between any pair of nodes from A and B typically share a long chain of common vertices, implying that the network distance between any pair of nodes from A and B is more or less the same. Based on this idea, a methodology is developed that defines *approximate distance oracles*, which can be used to find the approximate shortest path distance between any pair of nodes.

A similar idea [Sanders and Schultes, 2005] is to identify sequences of nodes via which a large number of shortest paths pass, similar to the intersections of highways in real road networks;

by creating shortcuts between highway nodes, shortest path search can be accelerated, by skipping over nodes that appear in the highways.

A number of variants to the shortest path query have been studied recently. Examples include multi-preference shortest path queries [Kriegel et al., 2010], where edge weights and path costs are aggregates of multiple measures on edges; the k-skip shortest path query [Tao et al., 2011], which computes a synopsis of a long shortest path; and shortest path queries with dynamic selections on allowable nodes and edges (e.g., avoid toll-roads) [Rice and Tsotras, 2010].

CHAPTER 6

Applications of Spatial Data Management Technology

In this chapter, we will discuss research areas closely related to spatial data management as well as areas where spatial database technology has been successfully applied to model and solve problems. This chapter is not meant to be exhaustive; the objective is to demonstrate the ample application of spatial data management techniques to other areas. Thus, although spatial data management started as an extension to relational databases to handle geospatial information, it has since evolved as a core area in database research with application in a wide range of data management and analysis problems.

We will start with the closely related field of spatio-temporal data management. Then, we will cover issues in indexing and searching high-dimensional data; a problem relevant to the management of complex objects in multimedia and time-series databases. The application of spatial indexing in searching and analyzing spaces of ranked objects based on user preferences will then be covered. Spatial data mining and OLAP are the next topics that will briefly be discussed. Finally, we will elaborate on the use of spatial indexing to solve data privacy problems and to extend traditional keyword search by considering the locations of the searched documents.

6.1 SPATIO-TEMPORAL DATA MANAGEMENT

Spatio-temporal data management has become an active research area. The objective is the efficient management of spatio-temporal data, such as trajectories of moving objects. Such data, nowadays, can routinely be collected with the help of GPS technology, stored, and analyzed. The temporal dimension introduces differences in the data model and query types, compared to snapshot spatial data, and new challenges for storage and indexing.

6.1.1 MODELS AND QUERIES FOR SPATIO-TEMPORAL DATA

Spatio-temporal data can be as simple as *timestamped events*. For example, consider a database relation storing emergency calls in a city tagged with a spatial location and a time-stamp. In this relation, every tuple (i.e., object) is associated with a three-dimensional value in the space-time 3D space. For such data, the third (temporal) dimension is no different in nature compared to the two spatial coordinates. Therefore, the data can simply be viewed as three-dimensional spatial objects. Storage and indexing can be performed as in the 2D case, to facilitate spatio-temporal selection queries. Such

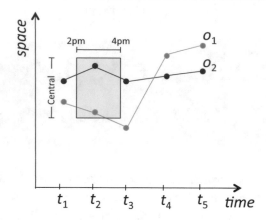

Figure 6.1: Examples of object trajectories in a Moving Objects Database.

queries specify ranges in the space and time dimensions, which can be combined to a 3D region. For example, query "find all emergency calls from Central district during 2am-4am yesterday" defines a 3D range which includes all locations in Central district during a time-range. Range queries can also be combined with nearest neighbor search. For example, the query "find the nearest emergency calls to the scene of crime during 2am-4am yesterday", performs a spatial nearest neighbor search, excluding events that fall outside the specified temporal selection range (2am-4am, yesterday).

Most commonly, however, spatio-temporal objects are not instantaneous spatial events, but entities with temporal duration. A *Moving Objects Database* (MOD) manages trajectories of moving objects in space (e.g., routes of cars, movements of animals, weather patterns, etc.). In a MOD, each object is modeled by a *sequence* of time-stamped spatial locations. For example, a moving car can be modeled by the sequence of its GPS-tracked positions. The sequence can become continuous in time, by interpolating the locations of consecutive timestamps. For example, assume that we know the exact positions l_i and l_{i+1} of a car at two consecutive GPS-tracked timestamps t_i and t_{i+1}. The unknown car's positions between t_i and t_{i+1} can be approximated by the points on the line segment connecting l_i and l_{i+1} (the timestamps for all locations on the segment are also interpolated). This is illustrated in Figure 6.1, where for trajectories of two objects o_1 and o_2, sampled at regular timestamps, the locations between the sampled points are modeled by interpolation. For the ease of visualization, one-dimensional projections of the spatial locations are shown in the figure. Spatio-temporal trajectories are often compressed by suppressing locations, which can approximately be inferred by interpolating the remaining points (i.e., by application of *line simplification* algorithms). For example, the location of object o_2 at time t_4 can be suppressed, since it can be inferred by the line segment connecting the points at times t_3 and t_4.

Given a MOD, *snapshot* spatio-temporal queries can be applied at any timestamp of the recorded history of the object trajectories, or at the predicted locations of future object locations.

As an example, consider the *historical* snapshot selection query, which asks for the cars that were in Central district at 2pm, yesterday. This query specifies a reference spatial region (Central district), a spatial predicate (inside) and a reference timestamp (2pm yesterday). We may also have *predictive* queries, e.g. "which cars are anticipated to be in Central district one hour from now?". For queries referring to the future, predictive models are used to estimate locations of objects (e.g., extrapolation, regression, autocorrelation, etc.)

Apart from snapshot queries, an MOD user may also pose *interval* queries, which have a reference time interval. For interval queries, the user may express a range of *spatio-temporal predicates* which stem from different combinations of spatial and temporal relationships. We have reviewed spatial relationships in Chapter 2. Temporal relationships between interval data are illustrated in Figure 6.2. The figure shows 7 relationships between two intervals x and y, based on their endpoints. For the first six of them, there also exists an inverse relationship (e.g., the inverse of *during* is *contains*), so the overall number of relationships is 13.

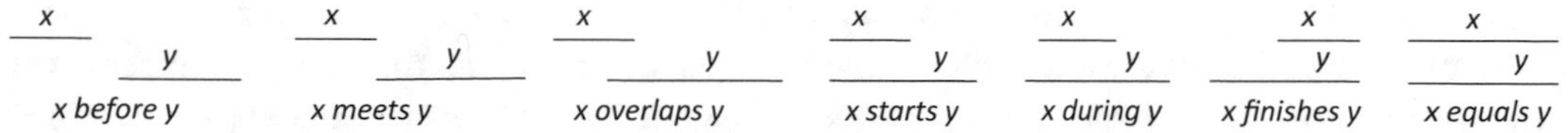

Figure 6.2: Temporal relationships between intervals based on their endpoints.

A spatio-temporal selection query is defined by a spatio-temporal range and a spatio-temporal predicate. For example, we may ask for cars that entered Central district *before* 2pm and left it *after* 4pm. The spatio-temporal range of this query is a 3D volume, bounded by Central district in space and by the interval [2pm, 4pm] in time. The query predicate requires that the qualified objects should be *contained* in the spatial range of the query (i.e., Central district) in *all* timestamps of the time interval. Figure 6.1 illustrates the query as a rectangle (the 2D Central region is shown as a 1D interval on the space axis here). Object o_2 qualifies the query because its trajectory remains within the spatial range of the query throughout the query time interval. On the other hand, observe that o_1 exits the spatial range before the end of the time interval; therefore, it is not a query result. The spatial region of a query does not necessarily remain constant throughout the temporal interval. Consider, for example, the spatio-temporal query "find all cars that came within a distance of 20 meters from car q at any time from 2pm to 4pm". In this query, the spatial region is a circle around car q and its position at every query timestamp in the [2pm, 4pm] query interval depends on the (changing) location of q over time. If a car is closer than 20 meters to q at any timestamp in [2pm, 4pm], then it is reported as a result.

Besides predictive queries that refer to the future and consider the anticipated movements of objects to derive their results, we may also have *continuous* spatial queries that refer to the present and future and require their evaluation at every change in the object positions. Unlike traditional *one-time* queries that are evaluated by a single search in the database, continuous queries remain valid for a long time and they are evaluated at every database update. An exemplary query in this class is "report any car that enters Central district from now and during the next two hours". The query does not use the predicted routes of objects to "guess" the ones that enter the spatial region in the next two hours, but it is continuously evaluated for the next two hours and reports any object that satisfies the spatial predicate at the time when this happens. In effect, the roles of the data and queries are reversed; when data are updated, the continuous queries that are affected by the changes should be found in order to update their results.

Time-parameterized queries can be used as components of continuous queries. They are executed at the present and predict when the query result will change in the future. When this happens, the query is issued again to update the result. More specifically, a time-parameterized query is a spatial query that is executed against the present state of the database and it computes (i) the result of the spatial query; (ii) the *validity period* of the result, given the current motion of data (and query) objects; and (iii) the anticipated *change* at the end of the validity period in the result. As an example, consider a user who wants to monitor all hotels within 10km distance from her current position. A time-parameterized query is issued to find the set of hotels (e.g., $\{h_1, h_2, h_3\}$) currently inside the 10km spatial range. The query also includes the time (e.g., 10 minutes) that this answer set is valid (given the direction and the speed of the user's movement), and the corresponding change in the result (e.g., 10 minutes later hotel h_2 is no longer within 10km from the user).

Another concept, also used in the evaluation of continuous queries, is the *safe region* of an object with respect to continuous spatial queries on dynamic data. Users issue continuous queries having their locations as reference against a set of moving objects. Instead of continuously checking whether the changes in the object locations affect the query results, for each object, we define a safe region. As long as the object's movement is confined within its safe region, no query results are affected by the changes in the object's location. As a simple example, consider a continuous query for the set of cars in Central district. For cars currently in Central district, the safe region is the district itself; as long as the cars stay within the district, there is no need for them to update their locations in the database. Similarly, for cars outside the district, the safe region is the space outside the district. Only cars that cross the city boundaries should update their positions in order for the continuous query result to be refreshed. If there are multiple continuous queries, the intersection of safe regions of all queries is used to define the ultimate safe region of an object.

6.1.2   INDEXING

Indexing methods for spatio-temporal data are divided into two classes: those that focus on queries that refer to the *past* movements of objects, stored in a database of trajectories, and those that refer to the *present and future* positions of objects, based on their anticipated movement.

Indexing trajectories of past movements

Indexes in the first category directly use or extend classic spatial access methods for trajectory data. The typical approach is to decompose the trajectory data into line segments; each line segment is modeled by the locations and timestamps of its endpoints, paired with the identifier of the object to which the trajectory belongs. The segments are then indexed by a 3D R–tree. A spatio-temporal query is then answered by retrieving the segments that qualify the spatio-temporal predicate. For example, consider again the query "find all cars that entered Central district before 2pm and left it after 4pm", illustrated in Figure 6.1. An R–tree search is applied to find the segments of the trajectories that intersect the [Central][2pm, 4pm] spatio-temporal query range. The segments are then post-processed and those belonging to the same object are brought together to form the part of the corresponding trajectory that intersects the query range. Finally, the objects that qualify the query are identified.

Note that in this 3D R–tree approach, the grouping of data is done at the line segment level. Therefore, a leaf node of the tree may store line segments from different trajectories that are close in the time-space domain and the line segments of a given trajectory may be distributed to multiple leaf nodes. Therefore, the data structure may not be efficient for spatio-temporal queries that require the traversal of a trajectory for a long time interval. An alternative access method that would be more efficient for such queries would strictly preserve trajectories, such that a leaf node only contains segments belonging to the same trajectory. The *Trajectory Bundle* tree (TB–tree for short) is an access method, similar to the 3D R–tree, which follows this requirement and stores the trajectory of an object in a linked list of leaf nodes. To answer our exemplary query using the TB–tree, we use the tree structure to find the trajectories that are in Central district at 2pm (i.e., a *snapshot* query), and then follow the links to the neighboring leaf nodes of qualifying trajectories to verify the spatio-temporal predicate for each candidate.

So far, we have assumed that the indexed objects move constantly in time. In fact, in many applications, objects remain stationary for long periods. For example, cars may stay parked for long periods of time. In addition, some types of spatio-temporal data are not moving objects, but events that appear, stay valid for some period, and then disappear, remaining on a constant location throughout their lifetimes (for example, buildings on a map). *Historical* and *multi-version* R–trees have been designed to index spatio-temporal data collections, which may also include stationary objects. Conceptually, one R–tree is defined for every timestamp of the indexed history; any part of the R–tree that does not change at two consecutive timestamps is shared between the corresponding materialized trees.

Indexing future positions

The second class of indexing methods target the efficient evaluation of spatio-temporal queries that refer to the future. Since precise information about the future locations of objects is unknown, indexing relies on estimates that are derived from the objects' current locations and velocities.

A characteristic index for spatio-temporal predictive queries is the TPR–tree. The TPR–tree is similar to the R–tree in that it hierarchically groups objects, aiming at minimizing the number of node accesses during search. However, the TPR–tree does not focus on indexing the current locations of objects only; it also indexes their velocities, capturing therefore their anticipated locations in the future. The basic information for every object o that is indexed is the object's current location $o.l$ (i.e., location at time 0) and the object's current velocity $o.v$. The location is a 2D vector, with one value per coordinate; similarly, the velocity is a 2D vector, with one value per dimensional projection. For example, Figure 6.3a shows the locations of three objects a, b, c at current time 0; e.g., $a.l = (7, 6)$. For each object, the velocity is modeled by a vector; e.g., $a.v = (-2, -2)$ implies that at each timestamp a is moving -2 units along the x-axis and -2 units along the y-axis. The locations of object a after one and two timestamps are denoted by a' and a'', respectively in Figure 6.3a. The TPR–tree is designed for a limited time horizon H in the future and, during this time, the velocities of objects are assumed to be constant. In other words, for up to H timestamps in the future, we use the current object locations and velocities to predict their future positions.

A leaf node of the TPR–tree indexes a set of objects, based on their locations and velocities. The node is represented by a *MOving Rectangle* (MOR), which includes an SBox and a VBox. The SBox is the MBR of all objects at time 0, while the VBox has the minimum and maximum object velocities at each interval. For example, Figure 6.3b shows the locations at time 0 and the velocities of four moving objects a, b, c, d. The four objects are divided into two groups stored into separate leaf nodes of the TPR–tree. The MORs of the two groups are M_1 (storing b, c) and M_2 (storing a, d). M_1 is the MBR of b, c at time 0; its velocity intervals at dimensions x and y are $[1, 1]$ and $[1, 2]$, respectively. The extend of the MOR at any time in the future (until H) is determined by adding to its lower (upper) dimensional projections at time 0 the product of the lower (upper) corresponding velocity interval with the timestamp. For example, Figure 6.3c shows the spatial extents of the MORs at time 1. Compared to Figure 6.3b, the lower y-bound of M_1 has moved 1 spatial unit, while the upper y-bound has moved 2 units, due to the velocity y-interval $[1, 2]$. Based on its definition, the MOR is guaranteed to enclose all objects indexed by it at any time in the future (assuming constant velocities).

The TPR–tree hierarchically groups objects and MORs, similar to the R–tree. Its insertion algorithm is similar to that of the R–tree. The objects are grouped into MORs, aiming at minimizing the average MOR extent at any time moment from 0 to $0 + H$. For example, in Figure 6.3b, objects a and b, although spatially close to each other, are not grouped together because they move at different directions and the MOR of such a group is expected to grow large faster than the MBR of the group $\{b, c\}$. Finally, a query is evaluated by traversing the tree and pruning MORs (and their respective sub-trees) that do not qualify the spatio-temporal predicate of the query.

Apart from the TPR–tree (and its optimized TPR*–tree version), several other predictive indexes have been proposed. The B^x–tree indexes only the current spatial locations of objects along a space-filling curve, while maintaining a histogram for the object velocities at the different areas of the spatial domain. To process a range query that refers to the future, the range of the query is extended according to the maximum velocities of objects around this region and the time-difference of the query to the current time. After this extension, the query range is guaranteed to include all object locations at current time that may be results of the query. The candidates are verified using their precise locations and velocities. The B^x–tree has very low update cost, so it is more appropriate

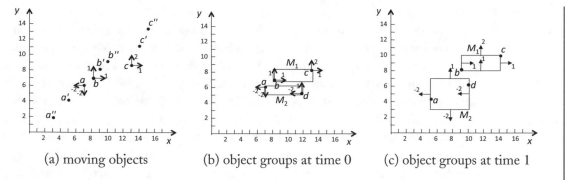

(a) moving objects   (b) object groups at time 0   (c) object groups at time 1

Figure 6.3: Illustration of objects' grouping by the TPR–tree.

for dynamic environments, compared to the TPR*–tree. STRIPES is another index, which instead of indexing the objects in the direct space-time domain, it represents each object as a point in the *dual*, space-velocity domain. In other words, instead of representing each object by a line connecting its locations over time, in the 3D space-time domain, the objects are 4D points in the space-velocity domain (i.e., the 2D location and velocity vectors). A bucket quadtree is used to index the 4D points and to evaluate queries (which are also transformed in the 4D space). The B^{dual}–tree is another index that applies the idea of the B^x–tree in the 4D dual space.

6.2   HIGH DIMENSIONAL DATA MANAGEMENT

Spatial data can be seen as a special case of multi-dimensional data. In many applications, objects are abstracted and modeled by feature vectors, which, in turn, can be seen as points in a high-dimensional feature space. In data mining, proximity in such a feature space is used to model the *similarity* between the corresponding objects. Databases of feature vectors are collected and indexed in order to support efficient search and analysis. There are two main differences between spatial data and feature vectors. First, spatial data are two or three dimensional, whereas the dimensionality of feature vectors can be arbitrarily high (typically, tens to hundreds of dimensions). Second, feature vectors do not have spatial extent; they are simple high-dimensional points. Although these differences are important enough to differentiate spatial data management from high-dimensional data management, the two problems have commonalities in modeling and query evaluation.

As an example, consider the problem of *content–based* image retrieval in image databases. In this problem, the user searches for images in a database which are *similar* to an input image. For example, a tourist may take a photo of a landmark in a city and ask for similar images in a public database in order to identify similar pictures and then find information about the landmark from these pictures. Typical content-based retrieval systems extract visual features (e.g., color, texture, etc.) from the images in the database and model each image as a high-dimensional feature vector. As an example, Figure 6.4 shows the extraction of a d-color histogram from an image, which, in turn, can be viewed as a d-dimensional point $p = (p_1, p_2, \ldots, p_d)$. The histogram stores for each of the d colors (or color-groups) the percentage of the color in the image pixels. Color histograms are convenient means for assessing similarity between multimedia objects. If two images are similar (by color), they should have similar histograms. Similar histograms correspond to points which are very close to each other in the high-dimensional space defined by the color bins. Thus, a multimedia query-by-example could be evaluated as follows. First, we extract all histograms for the known images in the database and create the corresponding set of high-dimensional points P. Then, for a particular user query image I_q, we compute the histogram q and search a set of points in P, which are close to q. These points correspond to images with similar colors as q, and as a result, these images will have high probability to be the desired results by the user. In practice, of course, color similarity search is combined with search based on other features (e.g., texture, spatial color layout, shapes, etc.) to narrow the set of candidate results or define a more appropriate ranking of the database objects with respect to their similarity to the query.

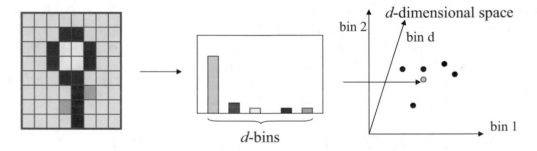

Figure 6.4: Color histogram and high-dimensional point representation of an image.

Besides content-based multimedial retrieval, there is a wide range of applications, where data objects are modeled as high-dimensional points and their proximity is used to assess similarity. In relational data, we can model every row of a table as a point in the multi-dimensional space defined by the table's attributes. In a text database, each document f can be modeled as a high-dimensional point $p(f)$, where every dimension i corresponds to a term and the i-th value of $p(f)$ is the frequency of the corresponding term in f. In a time-series database, each timestamp can be mapped to a dimension and each sequence can be modeled as a high-dimensional point in the domain of timestamp combinations.

6.2.1   SIMILARITY MEASURES AND QUERIES

As discussed, proximity between high-dimensional vectors is modeled with the help of a distance measure. Then, the problem of finding the most similar vectors to a given vector q from a database is equivalent to the problem of finding the nearest set of points to a query point in a high dimensional space. The most intuitive distance measure that we can use for this problem is the Euclidean distance.

Formally, given two d-dimensional vectors (i.e., points) p and q their Euclidean distance is defined by:

$$L_2(p, q) = \sqrt{\sum_{i=1}^{d} (p_i - q_i)^2},\tag{6.1}$$

where p_i is the value of p in the i-th dimension. In fact, the Euclidean distance is a specialization of the Minkowski distance metrics L_r:

$$L_r(p, q) = \left(\sum_{i=1}^{d} (p_i - q_i)^r\right)^{1/r}\tag{6.2}$$

This set of metrics satisfy the triangular inequality, which is a fundamental property for efficient indexing and searching. The Euclidean distance is a special case with $r = 2$; other popular specializations are the *Manhattan* (or *city-block*) distance with $r = 1$ and the *supremum* (or *infinity-norm*) distance with $r = \infty$. (The supremum distance is defined by $L_\infty(p, q) = \max_{i=1}^{d} |p_i - q_i|$.)

Let $\mathcal{P}$ be a collection of d-dimensional feature vectors (e.g., image histograms). Let $dist(p, s)$ be a distance measure that quantifies the dissimilarity between any pair of objects $p, s \in \mathcal{P}$. Similarity retrieval is often realized in the form of two query types.

- A *similarity range* query takes as input the feature vector of a query object q (e.g., the histogram of an example image) and a distance threshold ε and retrieves all points in $\mathcal{P}$ that are no further than ϵ to q. Here, ϵ is a parameter, used for search; the user can enlarge or decrease the search range based on the quantity and quality of the retrieved results.

- A *similarity ranking* query takes as input the feature vector of a query object q and an integer k and retrieves the set of k objects with the nearest feature vectors to the query vector q.

6.2.2   MULTI-DIMENSIONAL INDEXES AND THE CURSE OF DIMENSIONALITY

An intuitive method to support similarity retrieval would be to index the high dimensional vectors with the use of a multidimensional access method. In Chapter 3, we have studied the dominant access method for spatial data; the R–tree. The R–tree is in fact appropriate not only for indexing 2-dimensional data, but its structure, construction, and search algorithms can be straightforwardly extended for indexing points and bounding boxes of arbitrary dimensionality. A d-dimensional bounding box (used as search key) is defined by a vector $B = \{[l_1, u_1], [l_2, u_2], \ldots, [l_d, u_d]\}$ of d intervals, where interval $[l_i, u_i]$ is the range that the box covers in the i-th dimension. In other words, $[l_i, u_i]$ is the projection of B to i-th dimensional axis.

Multimedia feature vectors can be organized hierarchically into groups bounded by minimum bounding boxes to a d-dimensional R–tree, using the standard tree construction algorithms. Then, the range search and nearest neighbor algorithms for R–trees (described in Chapter 4) can be used to retrieve the nearest vectors to a query q in the feature space. Intuitively, if the R–tree achieves effective grouping of the objects, similarity search will be very efficient compared to linear scan.

Unfortunately, it turns out that the performance of multidimensional access methods degenerates with the increase of data dimensionality. Thus, for 10 or more dimensions searching for the nearest neighbor of a query vector q using an R–tree requires visiting almost all nodes of the tree, resulting in more page accesses than the simple linear scan algorithm. To make things worse, the majority of R–tree node accesses are random, since usually the nodes are stored at a random order in the disk (and visited at a random order by the nearest neighbors algorithms). Thus, even when the R–tree-based similarity search algorithms visit less nodes than the number of pages in a sequential file that stores the points, the actual I/O cost of the algorithms could be higher compared to the cost of a simple algorithm based on sequential scan.

Even though several specialized indexes have been proposed with better performance than the R–tree for high-dimensional data (e.g., the X–tree, the VA–file, and the A–tree), it is still a common belief that similarity search in high-dimensional spaces is a difficult and unsolved problem in its generic form. Some theoretical studies show that unless the high dimensional data are well-clustered or correlations exist between the dimensions, nearest neighbor search in high dimensional spaces may be meaningless. For some common data distributions (e.g., points have uniform and independent values in each dimension), the distance from a random query q to its nearest neighbor is not significantly smaller than the distance between q and the furthest point to q in the dataset. This phenomenon is known as the *curse of dimensionality*. For instance, the potential value combinations that a 100-dimensional vector can take are so many (D^{100}, where D is the domain of distinct values in each dimension) that the distance between any pair of random points in this space is within a very small range compared to the smallest (0) and greatest ($\sqrt{d \cdot D}$) possible distances. The reader can verify this by analysis or experimentation.

Another problem of spatial indexes (like the R–tree) is that they attempt to define a (hierarchical) space partitioning such that all partitions contain approximately the same number of points. The sparsity of high dimensional data causes the partitions to have large dead space and increased overlap. As a result, there are many partitions which either contain the query point, or are closer to it than its nearest neighbor and need to be visited. We have discussed in Chapter 4 that during nearest neighbor search, the optimal search algorithm has to visit at least the nodes whose MBR intersects the "nearest neighbor region" of q, i.e., the circle defined by q and the distance from its nearest neighbor. In a high dimensional space the corresponding hypersphere is likely to intersect most of the nodes of the tree structure, causing many random I/O accesses. Finally, note that the fanout of the R–tree nodes decreases with dimensionality. The size of an entry in the tree is proportional to dimensionality. Thus, if we fix the node size of a tree equal to a page size of the system, the number of entries that fit in a node decreases. This problem can be tackled by the introduction of "supernodes" that assign more than one disk pages to a tree node (the X–tree is an extension of the R–tree that uses this idea). Another solution is to compress the information in the non-leaf entries of the tree (this idea is used in the A–tree index, yet another extension of the R–tree for high dimensional data).

6.2.3   GEMINI: GENERIC MULTIMEDIA OBJECT INDEXING

As discussed, for many multimedia databases, using multi-dimensional access methods to index the feature space fails to outperform the simple linear scan algorithm. An alternative idea, called GEMINI, is to transform the high-dimensional vectors to low-dimensional points, by the use of a lossy *dimensionality reduction* technique, and then index the transformed points using a multi-dimensional index, like the R–tree. The rationale behind this approach is that if the distance between transformed points *approximates* the distance between the original vectors, the multi-dimensional index could be used to eliminate large parts of the vectors that could not be the nearest neighbors of q in the original space.

To understand the exact algorithm, we must first formalize the mapping from the high-dimensional feature space to a space of lower dimensionality. Let $\mathcal{P}$ be a collection of d-dimensional vectors (e.g., image histograms) and $dist()$ be a distance measure used to assess the dissimilarity between any pair of points in $\mathcal{P}$. Consider a multi-dimensional space with d' dimensions, such that $d' \ll d$ (e.g., $d = 100$, $d' = 3$). Let $M()$ be a mapping function, such that for every $p \in \mathcal{P}$, $M(p) = p'$, where p' is a d'-dimensional vector. By applying $M()$ to every $p \in \mathcal{P}$, we can convert $\mathcal{P}$ to a collection $\mathcal{P}'$ of d'-dimensional vectors. Let $dist'()$ be a distance function such that $\forall p, s \in \mathcal{P}$, $dist'(M(p), M(s)) = dist'(p', s') \leq dist(p, s)$. In simple words, $M()$ and $dist'()$ are selected such that the distance between two converted vectors to low dimensional points is no greater than the distance between the original points.

For example, let $d = 10$ and $d' = 2$. Let $M(p) = (\sum_{i=1}^{5} p_i/5, \sum_{i=6}^{10} p_i/5)$. In words, the first dimension of a transformed vector p' takes as value the average of the first 5 dimensions in the original vector p and the second dimension of p' is the average of the last 5 values of p. In addition, let $dist() = dist'() = L_2$, i.e., the Euclidean distance is used in both spaces to assess dissimilarity. It can be shown that for any pair (p, s) of 10-dimensional points, $dist'(p', s') \leq dist(p, s)$.

Similarity range queries in GEMINI

Assume that a user inputs a query image with vector q and a number ϵ and asks for all images $p \in \mathcal{P}$, which are within distance ϵ from q (similarity range query). This query can be evaluated in two steps, as shown in the algorithm of Figure 6.5.

function *Gemini Rtwostep*(Query q, Pointset $\mathcal{P}$, real ϵ)
1.   convert q to q' using the mapping function $M()$;
2.   apply a *range* search to find $\mathcal{C} = \{p' \in \mathcal{P}' : dist'(p', q') \leq \epsilon\}$;
3.   **for** each $p' \in \mathcal{C}$ **do**
4.   retrieve the corresponding point p from $\mathcal{P}$;
5.   **if** $(dist(p, q) < \epsilon)$ **then output** p;

Figure 6.5: A two-step algorithm for similarity range queries in GEMINI.

The *filter* step of the *Gemini Rtwostep* algorithm (Lines 1–2) is its key step. Instead of trying to find the most similar vectors to q in the original space, we convert q to a low-dimensional vector q', using $M()$ and then find the subset of $\mathcal{P}'$, which contains transformed vectors p' not further than ϵ from q'. Recall that each of the converted vectors p' corresponds to an original high dimensional vector p. The resulting set $\mathcal{C}$ after the filter step contains all low-dimensional vectors for which the corresponding high dimensional points could be part of the query result. In other words, there exists no $p \in \mathcal{P}$ for which $dist(p, q) \leq \epsilon$ and $p' \notin \mathcal{C}$. This can be proved by the lower bounding property $dist'(p', s') \leq dist(p, s)$, which holds for any pair of d-dimensional vectors p and s and their mappings $p' = M(p)$, $s' - M(s)$. Observe that if some $p' \notin \mathcal{C}$, then $\epsilon < dist'(p', q')$. In addition, $dist'(p', q') \leq dist(p, q)$. Thus, for each $p' \notin \mathcal{C}$, we know that $\epsilon < dist(p, q)$ and p is not a query result. On the other hand, $\mathcal{C}$ may contain vectors p', for which the corresponding high-dimensional vector p is not a query result (there may be $dist(p, q) > \epsilon$). Thus the filter step only retrieves candidate query results, which may then have to be validated using the actual vectors p in the *refinement* step (Lines 3–5).

You may now wonder, why is it useful to convert our high-dimensional data to low-dimensional data and perform the query evaluation in two steps. There are several reasons why this is working better than the linear scan algorithm. First, in the filter step, we perform distance computations on low-dimensional vectors. These computations are significantly cheaper compared to computations using the original high-dimensional vectors. For example, observe from Equation 6.1 that the cost for computing the Euclidean distance is linearly proportional to the number of dimensions d. For some more complex distance measures (e.g., time-series warping) the cost with respect to d is even higher. By reducing the whole set of objects $\mathcal{P}$ to only those whose transformation appears in $\mathcal{C}$, we hope to reduce the number of expensive exact distance computations ($\mathcal{C}$ is expected to be much smaller than $\mathcal{P}'$).

The second reason for this two-step query evaluation is that in the reduced dimensional space we have the option to apply fast, index-based search. Recall that multi-dimensional indexes are not appropriate for high-dimensional vectors. However, if d' is small enough, we can use a spatial access method (e.g., the R–tree) to index $\mathcal{P}'$. This will help us to evaluate the range search of the filter step very fast.

We now illustrate the functionality of the two-step similarity range search algorithm by an example. Consider a set $\mathcal{P} = \{a, b, c, d, e, f, g, h\}$ of 10-dimensional vectors, as shown on the left of Figure 6.6. Using the mapping function $M(p) = (\sum_{i=1}^{5} p_i/5, \sum_{i=6}^{10} p_i/5)$, described above, we can convert $\mathcal{P}$ to a set of 2-dimensional points $\mathcal{P}'$, which are shown in the figure in vector format. The points are also drawn on the right of the figure. Assume that $dist() = dist'() = L_2$, i.e., the distance function used in both spaces is the Euclidean distance. We can prove the lower bounding property $dist'(p', s') \leq dist(p, s)$, as already discussed. Now, consider the query vector q, also shown in the figure, and its low-dimensional mapping q'. Assume that we want to retrieve all vectors p in $\mathcal{P}$, such that $dist(p, s) \leq 2$. By applying the two-step algorithm, we first apply a 2-dimensional range query with radius 2 around q' and retrieve $\mathcal{C} = \{b', g'\}$. In the refinement step we validate the actual distances $dist(b, q)$ and $dist(g, q)$, from which only $dist(g, q) \leq 2$; thus, the only result of the query is g. Note that the refinement step is necessary since the evaluation of the query in the low dimensional space gives us more results than necessary. In addition, note that for processing the 2-dimensional range query in $\mathcal{P}'$, we could use an R–tree, which is very efficient for 2-dimensional vectors.

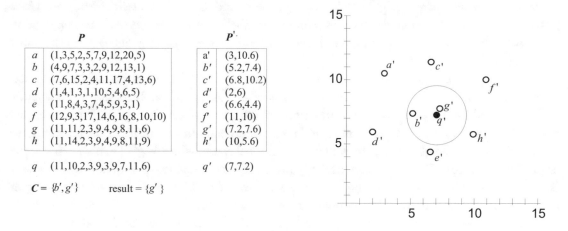

	P
a	(1,3,5,2,5,7,9,12,20,5)
b	(4,9,7,3,3,2,9,12,13,1)
c	(7,6,15,2,4,11,17,4,13,6)
d	(1,4,1,3,1,10,5,4,6,5)
e	(11,8,4,3,7,4,5,9,3,1)
f	(12,9,3,17,14,6,16,8,10,10)
g	(11,11,2,3,9,4,9,8,11,6)
h	(11,14,2,3,9,4,9,8,11,9)

	P'
a'	(3,10.6)
b'	(5.2,7.4)
c'	(6.8,10.2)
d'	(2,6)
e'	(6.6,4.4)
f'	(11,10)
g'	(7.2,7.6)
h'	(10,5.6)

q (11,10,2,3,9,3,9,7,11,6)

q' (7,7.2)

$\mathcal{C} = \{b', g'\}$ result $= \{g'\}$

Figure 6.6: Example of a two-step similarity range query.

Similarity ranking queries in GEMINI

Given a query image with vector q and a number k, a ranking query retrieves the set of k images whose vectors are closer to q than any other vector in the collection $\mathcal{P}$. The two-step algorithm we saw in Section 6.2.3 can be adapted for ranking queries as shown in Figure 6.7.

function $Gemini\,NN\,twostep$(Query q, Pointset $\mathcal{P}$, int k)
1.   convert q to q' using the mapping function $M()$;
2.   compute $\mathcal{NN}$: the set of k nearest neighbors of q' in $\mathcal{P}'$;
3.   **for** each $s' \in \mathcal{NN}$ **do**
4.   retrieve the corresponding vector $s \in \mathcal{P}$;
5.   compute $dist(s, q)$;
6. $\epsilon := maximum\ dist(s, q), \forall s' \in \mathcal{NN}$;
7.   apply a *range* search to find $\mathcal{C} = \{p' \in \mathcal{P}' : dist'(p', q') \leq \epsilon\}$;
8.   **for** each $p' \in \mathcal{C}$ **do**
9.   retrieve the corresponding point p from $\mathcal{P}$ and compute $dist(p, q)$;
10. **output** the set of k points with the smallest $dist(p, q)$;

Figure 6.7: A two-step algorithm for similarity ranking queries in GEMINI.

The filter step (Lines 1–7 in Figure 6.7) of the ranking algorithm, retrieves a set of candidate points $\mathcal{C}$ as in the similarity range search case. However, the retrieval of these points is based on a different procedure. First, we retrieve $\mathcal{NN}$: the set of k nearest neighbors of q' in $\mathcal{P}'$. For every point s' in $\mathcal{NN}$, we compute the actual distance $dist(s, q)$ in the original space and set as ϵ the maximum of these distances. Now, we know that there are k points in $\mathcal{P}$ with distance at most ϵ from q; however, there could be other points in-between, so we are not sure if this is the set of actual nearest neighbors. What we know for sure is that there can be no vector p in the response set, such that $dist'(p', q') > \epsilon$. Thus, we use bound ϵ to search in the low-dimensional for the candidates $\mathcal{C}$ that could be the nearest neighbors. For each of these candidates, in the refinement step (Lines 8–10), we compute the actual distances to q and return the set of k closest ones. The computation of the k closest points in this step can be assisted with the help of a priority queue, as in the linear search algorithm.

The algorithm does not miss any results because of the lower-bounding condition $dist'(p', s') \leq dist(p, s)$. Note that the computations of $\mathcal{NN}$ and $\mathcal{C}$ can be performed efficiently if $\mathcal{P}'$ is indexed by an R–tree, using the algorithms of Chapter 4. Consider again the example data of Figure 6.6, and assume that we want to find the nearest neighbor of q in $\mathcal{P}$. In the filter step, we retrieve the nearest neighbor of q' in the low-dimensional space, which is g'. Then we retrieve the original vector g from $\mathcal{P}$ and compute $dist(g, p) = \sqrt{3}$. Since, we are looking for only one neighbor $(k = 1)$, $\epsilon = dist(g, p) = \sqrt{3}$. Using this range we search around q' in $\mathcal{P}'$ and retrieve no other point than g', thus g is eventually output as the nearest neighbor.

It turns out, however, that the two-step approach described above is not the best possible for ranking queries in GEMINI. The reason is that search is based on the k nearest neighbors in $\mathcal{P}'$, the actual distances of which in the high-dimensional space could be arbitrary. Thus, the greatest actual distance of those neighbors, which is used for search could be very large, resulting in a very large candidate set $\mathcal{C}$ to be validated. A better approach is to *incrementally* retrieve nearest neighbors in the low-dimensional space and refine the set of k actual nearest neighbors found so far, until the next nearest neighbor in the low-dimensional space has distance no smaller than the k-th closest actual distance found so far. This multi-step approach is described by the algorithm of Figure 6.8.

function $GeminiNNmultistep($Query q, Pointset $\mathcal{P}$, int $k)$
1.   convert q to q' using the mapping function $M()$;
2.   Initialize max-heap H with k $\langle NULL, \infty \rangle$ entries;
3.   **while** there are more neighbors of q' in $\mathcal{P}'$ **do**
4. $p' :=$ next neighbor of q' in $\mathcal{P}'$; /* apply *incremental* NN retrieval */
5.   **if** $dist'(p', q') \geq top(H).dist)$ **then**
6.   **goto** Line 11; /* termination condition */
7.   retrieve point p from $\mathcal{P}$ and compute $dist(p, q)$;
8.   **if** $(dist(p, q) < top(H).dist)$ **then**
9. $top(H):=\langle p, dist(p, q) \rangle$;
10.   max-heapify$(top(H))$;
11.   **return** H;

Figure 6.8: A multi-step algorithm for similarity ranking queries in GEMINI.

Algorithm $GeminiNNmultistep$ incrementally retrieves the nearest neighbors of p' in $\mathcal{P}'$. For each such point, it loads the corresponding high-dimensional vector and computes its actual distance to q. The set of k-closest actual points during this process are maintained in the heap H.

The algorithm terminates (Line 5) as soon as a retrieved neighbor p' in $\mathcal{P}'$ has no smaller distance to q' than the actual distance of the k-th nearest neighbor found so far. In this case, we know that for p' and all remaining points in $\mathcal{P}'$ the actual vectors may not be closer to q than the k nearest neighbor set we have found so far (which is kept in H). This is guaranteed by the lower-bounding condition $dist'(p', s') \leq dist(p, s)$ and by the fact that low-dimensional vectors p' are retrieved incrementally from $\mathcal{P}'$ based on their distance to q'. The reader can prove the correctness of this algorithm as an exercise.

$GeminiNNmultistep$ minimizes the number of objects, which we need to access from $\mathcal{P}$ and compute their actual distance to q, at the expense of potentially accessing more objects from $\mathcal{P}'$ (in order of their closeness to q'), compared to $GeminiNNtwostep$. This trade-off pays off, since every access to $\mathcal{P}$ causes a random I/O, and it is significantly more important to minimize them as opposed to accesses to $\mathcal{P}'$, which can be performed cheaply with the help of a spatial index (e.g., R–tree) and an incremental NN search algorithm (like the best-first algorithm described in Chapter 4). In addition, computations of $dist'()$ using the points in $\mathcal{P}'$ are significantly less expensive than computations of $dist()$ for the exact points. Thus $GeminiNNmultistep$ is much more efficient than $GeminiNNtwostep$, in practice.

Dimensionality reduction techniques

The GEMINI approach requires the definition of an appropriate mapping function $M()$ to define $\mathcal{P}$. Mapping a high-dimensional vector to a low-dimensional point is often called *dimensionality reduction*. Several dimensionality reduction techniques can be used for this conversion. Many of these techniques originate from signal processing and were used to compress long sequences of values that exhibit periodicity, by a mixture of simple functions. An example of such a technique is the *Discrete Fourier Transform*, which represents a sequence of values as a linear combination of sines and cosines. By using only a few of the first (most significant) coefficients, we can approximate the vector by a small number of values (i.e., a low-dimensional vector). It turns out that the approximation satisfies the lower bounding property $dist'(p', s') \leq dist(p, s)$ most common L_p distance metrics $dist'()$ and $dist()$; therefore, it is appropriate for GEMINI.

Additional dimensionality reduction techniques include the Discrete Wavelet Transform, the Singular Value Decomposition, the Piecewise Linear Approximation, etc. The applicability and effectiveness of different techniques depends on the domain of the converted vectors and the distance measure $dist()$ in the primary space.

6.3   MULTI-CRITERIA RANKING

Ranking has become a standard component in database systems. Users are often interested in ranking objects (or database tuples) with respect to their values on some attributes. For example, the ORDER BY clause is often used in SQL expressions to sort the result of a query in some attribute-based ascending or descending order. Information systems and search engines often apply *multi-criteria* ranking of objects by combining rankings based on different features. For example, to evaluate a keyword query, a meta-search engine aggregates rankings from different engines to generate a combined ranking of documents. In multimedia information systems, similarity search based on different criteria (e.g., textual tags, visual content, etc.) generate different rankings for images, which can then be combined to generate a single aggregated ranking.

In single- or multi-criteria object ranking, typically the user is not interested in the complete ranked list of objects, but only in the highly ranked ones. For example, in the multi-criteria multimedia search example, we are typically interested in the top-k images based on the global ranking. This is similar to k nearest neighbor search in spatial databases, where users are interested only in the k nearest objects to a given location. k nearest neighbor search can be viewed as a special case of top-k retrieval, where the only search criterion is the distance to a reference object. In a database system, a top-k query is expressed with the help of the ORDER BY clause, which specifies the ranking function, and the LIMIT (or STOP AFTER) clause, which limits the number of top-ranked tuples to be returned.

Another way to limit the objects to be selected is not to specify a limiting condition (i.e., top-k), but to compare the relative ranks of objects in all criteria (i.e., dimensions), and to return only the set of objects that are not *dominated* by others in all rankings. More specifically, consider a set of objects D and consider the d attributes of these objects that are used for ranking as dimensions. Without loss of generality, assume that smaller values are preferred to large ones in each dimension. If for an object $x \in D$, x_i represents x's value on the i-th ranking attribute, we say that object x dominates object y, if $x_i \leq y_i$ in every dimension i and there is some dimension j, such that $x_j < y_j$. In simple words x dominates y if it is no worse than y in all ranking criteria and better than y in at least one. For example, consider a set of hotels, for which the ranking criteria are (i) the price and (ii) the distance to the beach. Every hotel can be modeled as a two-dimensional (price, distance) vector and hotel x dominates hotel y if x's price and distance are both at most equal to those of y, while x has a strictly smaller price or distance than y. Intuitively, dominance defines a partial order on the objects based on multiple criteria: if x dominates y, then x would definitely be preferable to y by a user who selects based on these criteria. The set of objects in D, which are not dominated by any other object in D are the *skyline* of D. Thus, the skyline operator presents to the user only the superior objects, according to the ranking criteria. Therefore, as opposed to top-k search, the skyline query is a *parameter-free* operator that requires neither an aggregate function nor a limiting condition.

As an example of top-k and skyline search, consider a set of objects (e.g., hotels) as two-dimensional points in the price-distance space as illustrated in Figure 6.9a. A user may combine the price and distance values of each hotel by a *weighted sum* function to define a multi-criteria total order. For example, the use of function $2\times$price+distance, defines the order $h_5, h_6, h_7, h_3, h_4, h_8, h_2, h_1$. This order is equivalent to the order in which the dashed line with visit the points when swept in the direction of the arrow. By *limiting* the search only to the top-3 objects, the user retrieves hotels h_5, h_6, h_7, which are the best ones when giving double importance to the price compared to the distance. Alternative aggregate functions generate different orderings. Top-k queries provide flexibility to the users to select their criteria and define custom-based aggregate functions. The skyline query is appropriate for users who do not wish to define an aggregate function or a limiting condition, but they want to browse only the superior objects based on their preferences in the different dimensions. For example, for users that prefer cheap hotels close to the beach, the best set of hotels, is the skyline $\{h_1, h_5, h_6, h_7\}$, which contains the objects that are not dominated by others. For example, h_2 is not included in the skyline because it is dominated by h_5. Intuitively, a user would never choose h_5 instead of h_2, because h_2 is better than h_5 in terms of both price and distance.

6.3.1   TOP-k AND SKYLINE EVALUATION USING SPATIAL ACCESS METHODS

Classic approaches for top-k evaluation, assume that the object rankings with respect to the different criteria have already been generated or they are dynamically generated by an application interface. The goal of these approaches is to aggregate the different rankings of objects efficiently, in order to compute their global ranking according to the aggregate function and output the top-k objects there. For example, consider a database storing information about restaurants and assume that a user is interested in the top-10 restaurants in terms of price and food quality. The database can use a base ranking operation that outputs the restaurants in increasing price order and another operation that outputs them in decreasing order of food quality. Top-k aggregation runs on top and combines the outputs of the two base ranking operations in order to produce a global ranking and select the top-k objects in it.

Spatial database technology has been used to accelerate top-k search. Note that the top-k search problem can be modeled as a spatial search problem, as illustrated in the example of Figure 6.9a. If we model the objects as points in the multidimensional ranking space as illustrated in the figure, top-k search translates to a *line sweeping* problem; the objective is to find the first k objects to be swept by the line defined by the aggregation function, starting from the best point in space (the origin of axes in our example) and swept towards the worst point (defined the maximum values in all dimensions). This problem can be solved efficiently with the help of a spatial access method like the R–tree. Assume that we have indexed all points, representing hotels in this example, by an R–tree, taking as dimensions price and distance to the beach, as illustrated in Figure 6.9b. For the ease of illustration, we show a very simple tree where each node has a fanout of 2. The top-k query can be evaluated efficiently, with the help of a *best-first* top-k search, similar to the BF k-NN algorithm discussed in Section 4.2.2. This time, the R–tree entries are prioritized based on the order by which they are swept by the aggregate function f. Therefore, initially, we put in a priority queue Q the root entries $\{M_1, M_2\}$. The first entry to be de-heaped is M_2 because among all entries in Q its lower-left corner gives the lowest value to f. Note that the lowest-left corner of an MBR represents the best possible position for any point indexed under this MBR, with respect to their f values. This holds for any aggregate function f, which monotonically increases by increasing the values of its components. After M_2 is de-heaped, the R–tree node pointed by it is visited and its entries m_3 and m_4 are added to Q. Next, m_3 is de-heaped and h_5, h_6 are accessed and en-heaped. The next element of Q to be visited is h_5, which is guaranteed to be the top-1 object of f. The object is output and the algorithm continues until k objects are de-heaped. This algorithm is I/O optimal (with respect to the R–tree indexing) because it visits the minimal number of tree nodes required to guarantee the correctness of the top-k result.

A best-first algorithm can similarly be designed for skyline retrieval. This time, the MBRs and points are visited increasing distance order from the best point o (i.e., the origin of both axes). Due to the monotonicity of the distance function with respect to the scalar values, if $dist(o, h_i) \leq dist(o, h_j)$, then it is not possible for h_j to dominate h_i. Therefore, if we apply best-first NN search using o as the query point, it is guaranteed that the first object to be deheaped is a skyline point. After retrieving the first skyline point in this way (i.e., h_5), we use it to prune from the queue Q all entries that are dominated by it. In addition, we never enheap an entry that is dominated by points in the skyline S so far. An MBR m_i is dominated by a point h_j if the lower-left corner of m is dominated by h_j. In this case all points in m_i are guaranteed to be dominated by h_j. Continuing our example, once h_5 is deheaped and inserted to S as the only current skyline point, the heap contents are $\{h_6, m_4, M_1\}$. None of these entries is dominated by h_5, so search continues. The next entry to be deheaped is M_1. From the two entries m_1, m_2 in the R–tree node pointed by M_1, m_2 is eliminated because it is dominated by the current skyline $S = \{h_5\}$; on the other hand, m_1 is enheaped. The next deheaped element is h_6, which is guaranteed to be a skyline point (otherwise it would have been pruned). Thus, S is updated to $\{h_5, h_6\}$. Next, m_4 is visited, h_7 is inserted to S, and h_8 is pruned. Finally, m_1 is visited and the last skyline point h_1 is discovered (while h_2 is pruned due to h_5).

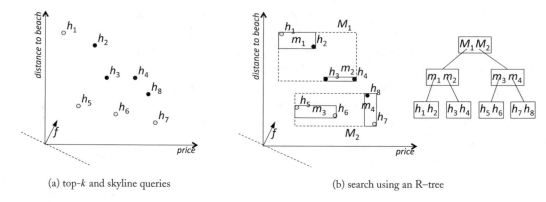

(a) top-k and skyline queries   (b) search using an R–tree

Figure 6.9: Top-k and skyline query evaluation using spatial access methods.

6.3.2   SPATIALLY RANKING DATA

We already observed that k-NN search is a special case of top-k search, using distance to a single reference point as the ranking criterion. By considering multiple reference points, k-NN search can be extended to *aggregate* k-NN search. As an example, consider a set of mobile users that wish to meet at a restaurant. The candidate restaurants where the users can meet can be ranked according to an aggregate distance to all users. For example, we can take the sum of distances to all users or the minimum distance to any user as the global (aggregate) ranking criterion. To evaluate an aggregate k-NN query over spatial data that are indexed by an R–tree, again we can use a best-first algorithm that prioritizes visits to the R–tree entries according to the best possible aggregate distance of any point in them. The details are left as an exercise to the reader.

In the same spirit of aggregate k-NN search, a *spatial skyline* query can be defined. Consider again a set of mobile users that wish to meet. A restaurant r_1 is definitely worse that another restaurant r_2, if for every user r_1 is further than r_2; i.e., r_2 *spatially dominates* r_1. The spatial skyline is the set of restaurants that are not dominated by others. Again, best-first search can be used to compute the spatial skyline, on top of important observations, such as the fact that all data inside the convex hull of the query points should be part of the skyline.

6.4   DATA MINING AND OLAP

In Section 6.2, we already discussed that data objects can be represented as high-dimensional feature vectors. Classic data mining tasks (like classification) can then be modeled as geometric problems in the high-dimensional space. In the following, we discuss a number of cases, where spatial data management technology can be used for data mining tasks.

6.4.1   CLASSIFICATION

Consider a database with a set of *training data* records, where there is one designated *class* attribute. The goal of classification is to build a model that predicts the value of the class attribute, given the values of other attributes with high accuracy. The data can be modeled as points in the high-dimensional space defined by the non-class attributes; the points are labeled by their class attribute values. Classification can then be considered as a geometric problem. The goal is to find regions in space defined by ranges in the attribute domains, such that these regions are as large as possible (model simplicity) and their contents are as *pure* as possible, with respect to the distribution of class labels in them (i.e., the great majority of records in these regions have the same class label). Such regions can take the label of the majority in them and can be used as classification rules. In fact, decision-tree classifiers follow this logic, by dividing the multidimensional space into partitions, based on the purity of the class labels in them. The space partitioning by a decision tree resembles the partitioning of spatial data points by a k-d-tree. Support vector machines also follow a similar logic by dividing the space using (not essentially rectilinear) lines, according to the purity of the partitions. Spatial indexing can be used to assist the identification of 'pure' regions that can define the classification rules. Finally, (lazy) instance-based classifiers, which determine the unknown class label of a sample, based on the sample's proximity to labeled instances, can directly make use of spatial indexes; for example, k-NN classifiers select the k nearest labeled points in the high-dimensional space and determine the label of the sample by (weighted) voting.

6.4.2 CLUSTERING

Clustering is the task of dividing a set of objects into groups, such that the similarity between objects in the same group is high, and objects that belong to different groups are dissimilar. As already discussed, after modeling objects as high-dimensional feature vectors, similarity is computed with the help of a distance measure. Therefore, clustering can also be thought as a geometric problem. Spatial data management techniques can be used to speed-up clustering. For example, if we index the objects using an R–tree, the structure of the tree can be used to guide clustering. The geometric centroids of the tree nodes can be used to approximate the data distribution. These can be used as cluster centroid seeds for classic *partitioning-based* clustering algorithms, such as k-means. In addition, spatial indexing can be used to accelerate the iterations of k-means, with the help of nearest neighbor retrieval around the current cluster centroids. Ideas that stem from spatial indexing have been employed in *hierarchical* clustering. For example, the BIRCH algorithm constructs a clustering feature tree, which summarizes the hierarchical data distribution and resembles the R–tree. Finally, *density-based* algorithms, like the classic DBSCAN, utilize spatial indexes to identify and connect dense regions of points, based on spatial range searching.

6.4.3 ASSOCIATION RULES MINING

Mining association rules identifies correlations between combinations of items or values in records. For example, in a database that stores combinations of items purchased in each customer transaction, an association rule could be "if a customer buys milk and diapers then he is also likely to buy beer with high probability". Rules can be extended to include associations that are governed by spatial relationships. For example, a spatial association rule could be "houses near the beach are likely to be expensive". This rule associates the fact that an object (house) satisfies a spatial relationship to a reference object (beach) to the object's value in another attribute (price). Mining rules that involve the geometric features of objects and spatial relationships can be facilitated by spatial access methods (which can direct the search according to the spatial predicate). In addition, there is a special class of *spatial collocation* rules, which identify spatial associations between classes of spatial objects or features. An example of such a rule is "90% of the kindergartens have a park within 200 meters from their location". Identification of spatial collocations can be done with the help of spatial join algorithms; by spatially joining the object collections (e.g., kindergartens, parks, etc.), we can find the percentage of pairs (or combinations) that are in the same spatial neighborhood and define collocation rules, if this percentage is of statistical significance.

6.4.4 SPATIAL AGGREGATION AND ON-LINE ANALYTICAL PROCESSING

Data warehouses integrate, summarize, and archive very large collections of historical operational data. The database schema of a warehouse is centered around a measurable subject. For example, the sale transactions of a corporation are collected and summarized at the most desirable detail level. In addition, a number of *dimension* along which it is desirable to analyze the data are determined (e.g., time, product, location, etc.). Figure 6.10 illustrates an exemplary schema for a data warehouse, which stores historical information about the product sales of a company. The central (sales) table is called the *fact* table. The fact table stores the summarized sales information at the most detailed level. For each combination of time, product, supplier, and location values, if there are any sales for that combination, a corresponding record appears in the fact table, accumulating the total number of sales is stored in the quantity attribute. The other tables are called *dimensional* tables and include detailed information for every unit of time, product, supplier, or location that appears in the fact table. The dimensional tables are linked with the fact table, via foreign key constraints (e.g., time_key in the sales table is a foreign key pointing to the time table).

On-Line Analytical Processing (OLAP) refers to the online progressive computation and visualization of summarized information from the data warehouse by means of GROUP BY queries. For example, a data analyst may be interested in viewing the total number of sales for each month in 2010 and for each product type. This information can be derived by joining the fact table with the time and product tables, selecting only tuples where the year is 2010, perform a group by (month, prod_type) and then display the sum(quantity) for each group. Apart from group-by queries, analysts may also pose CUBE BY queries. This construct computes and presents multiple group-by queries, for each subset of the selected dimensions. For example, a 'cube by' product and year query could produce the 2D *data cube* displayed in Figure 6.11; observe that for each of the four subsets of the (product, year) dimensions set, for all combinations of values the total number of sales are summarized and displayed. Each subset (and the values displayed) is called a *cuboid*. A data cube can have as high dimensionality as the number of dimensions and each dimension can be viewed at different granularities (e.g., day, month, year, for time). It is also possible to include selection conditions (e.g., display only months of 2010).

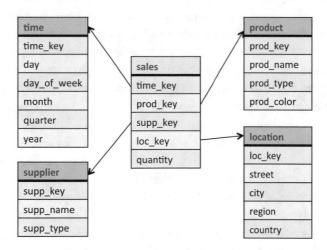

Figure 6.10: The (star) schema of a data warehouse.

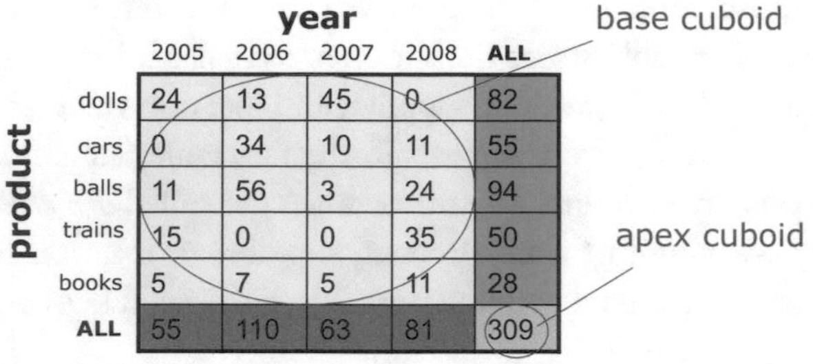

	2005	2006	2007	2008	ALL
dolls	24	13	45	0	82
cars	0	34	10	11	55
balls	11	56	3	24	94
trains	15	0	0	35	50
books	5	7	5	11	28
ALL	55	110	63	81	309

Figure 6.11: A data cube.

Observe that the data stored in a warehouse are multidimensional. Every record in the fact table can be modeled as a point, which takes as coordinates the key values of the records and also carries a measure value (sales quantity in our example). Spatial indexing can be used to facilitate the computation of OLAP queries. For example, if an OLAP query involves selections in the dimensional attributes, the query can be modeled as a spatial range query, which can be evaluated with the help of a spatial index. In addition, a data cube can be precomputed and indexed by a spatial access method. In practice, if there are multiple dimensions, the data cube is sparse (i.e., most of its cells are empty). Non-empty cells can be modeled as points (carrying measures) and can be indexed. If the result of an OLAP query can be derived from the data cube, then the index can be used to efficiently compute it. For example, if the data cube shown in Figure 6.11 is materialized and indexed by an R–tree, then the OLAP query "show the total number of doll sales in 2007-2008" can be modeled as a spatial range query (covering cells 45 and 0 in the first row), which can be evaluated using the R–tree.

More often than not, one of the dimensions in a data warehouse is spatial (for example, location in the schema of Figure 6.10). Like in any other dimension, a predefined hierarchy for locations can be used to analyze the data at different spatial granularity. For example, the data in the warehouse of Figure 6.10 can be analyzed at the levels of street, city, region, and country (e.g., an OLAP query could group the sales by city, while another could group them by street). However, in some applications the desired spatial granularity for analysis could be arbitrary. For example, it might be desirable to analyze information on spatial maps at arbitrary granularity levels, determined by zooming functions controlled by users. In addition, the user may perform arbitrary spatial *range aggregate* queries, which request for summary information in arbitrary spatial regions of the maps (e.g., "find the total number of sales within 100km from the competitor's department store"). For these cases, a predefined spatial hierarchy may not be adequate. This issue can be addressed with the help of a spatial index for data measures. Consider a set of measures (e.g., sales quantities) modeled as points on a spatial map. In order to support efficient aggregation of these values for arbitrary spatial ranges, we can construct an *aggregate* R–tree (aR–tree for short), which indexes these points, like a common R–tree, but includes aggregate information in intermediate node entries, which summarizes the data pointed in the corresponding subtrees.

Figure 6.12 illustrates a set of points $p_1 \ldots p_8$ and an aR–tree built on top of them. Observe that each indexed point is augmented with some measure information, denoted by the parentheses following the point in the tree leaf nodes. For example, point p_1 is associated with value 2. Observe that each intermediate node entry e also carry values; this value is a summary of the values of all entries in the node pointed by e. For example, the value of m_1 is 5; i.e., the *sum* of values of p_1 and p_2. The aR–tree borrows its construction and update methods from the R–tree, i.e., points are grouped to nodes solely based on their spatial features. The tree can be used to answer range aggregate queries, similar to the way the R–tree is used to evaluate range queries. The only difference is that if the MBR of an entry e is *entirely included* in the spatial range, then the aggregate value of e is directly accumulated in the query result and there is no need to access the corresponding subtree. This way, the aR–tree saves node accesses compared to the R–tree. For example, consider the circular range query Q shown in Figure 6.12. To answer this query, we first access the root node of the tree. Entry M_1 is pruned because it does not intersect Q. Entry M_2 partially intersects Q, so the node pointed by it is visited. Entry m_3 partially intersects Q; therefore, the leaf node pointed by it is visited and the measure of p_6 (which is inside the range) is added to the query result. Entry m_4 is totally included in the range Q; therefore, we do not have to access the corresponding leaf node; we just add m_4's aggregate value (i.e., 2) to the query result. The search algorithm terminates reporting 3 (i.e., 1 from p_6 + 2 from m_4). The tree can also be used to answer spatial group-by queries, where the domain of locations is arbitrarily partitioned into regions (e.g., using another spatial relation) and for each region an aggregate measure has to be computed. In this case, the aR–tree is *spatially joined* with the partitioning to derive the aggregate score for each region. Note that the tree of Figure 6.12 is a *sum* aR-tree (i.e., the aggregate function used in intermediate node entries is sum). Alternative (distributive or algebraic) functions (e.g., *count, max, min*) and combinations of them can also be used.

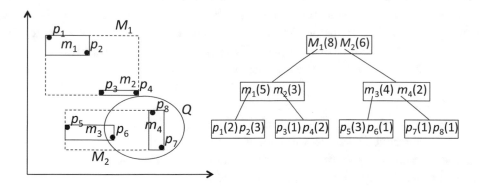

Figure 6.12: A set of points with measures and an aggregate *sum* R–tree.

6.5   PRIVACY-PRESERVING PUBLICATION OF MICRODATA

The goal of privacy-preserving data publishing is to make databases available to the public, while protecting any private information that exists in the data. As an example, consider a hospital, which maintains a database of patient records and wishes to publish this database in order to help researchers and other organizations to analyze the data. For example, an insurance company may be interested in finding patterns between the demographic features of patients and their diseases (e.g., people of age higher than 50, who live in Central district have higher chances for cancer compared to other population groups).

A straightforward way of publishing such hospital microdata would be to just remove the explicit identifiers (e.g., patient names) and publish the remaining information. For example, Figure 6.13a illustrates a simple table containing patient records, after removal of explicit identifiers of the patients. However, by publishing this information, there is a high risk of privacy breach by linking it with public data, which contain identification information for persons (e.g., telephone directories, public voters tables, facebook data, etc.) For example, if there is a unique person aged 70, who lives in the region with zipcode 13145, then this person can directly be linked to the 8th tuple of the table of Figure 6.13a and the disease of the person (Alzheimer's) is immediately revealed. This example illustrates that there may be a combination of attributes (age, zipcode, in our example), which can be used as a *quasi-identifier* (QID) for persons. When publishing sensitive information, it is imperative to protect the data from privacy attacks, which use QIDs to link sensitive information with real persons.

A solution to linkage attacks is to *generalize* the quasi-identifier data, prior to publication. For example, the hospital publishes the table of Figure 6.13b, where the exact values of QID attributes in tuples are replaced by generalized ranges. In this example, due to this generalization, any QID value (e.g., age=35, zipcode=13024) is linked to either 0 or at least 3 records in the published table. We say that this table satisfies 3-anonymity because of this property. In general, k-*anonymity* requires that any QID that can be linked to the published table, should be linked to at least k records. In effect, the record of a patient cannot be distinguished from at least $k - 1$ other records.

k-anonymity may not be sufficient if there is not enough diversity in the sensitive values of an anonymized group. For example, in Figure 6.13b, if we know that Bob, aged 25, whose address (zipcode) is 13012, visited the hospital, we may infer directly that Bob has gastritis, because in all records of the group, where the quasi-identifier (25, 13013) is linked to (i.e., the first group), the sensitive value is gastritis. To address this issue, a stricter privacy requirement should be used when grouping and generalizing records prior to publication. l-*diversity* requires that the probability of each sensitive value that appears in any group should not exceed $1/l$. For example, the groups in Figure 6.13b are l-diverse.

After generalizing quasi-identifiers in order to achieve k-anonymity or l-diversity, naturally the data lose some of their initial value. Some of the published values are no longer accurate, but they correspond to ranges in the domain of the corresponding attribute. In order to keep as much information as possible in the published data, an anonymization technique should minimize the

age	zipcode	disease
35	13024	gastritis
40	13112	pneumonia
20	13002	gastritis
25	13013	gastritis
60	13012	Alzheimer
55	13114	diabetes
60	13022	flu
70	13012	Alzheimer
50	13145	pneumonia

(a) original data

age	zipcode	disease
[20-35]	130*	gastritis
[20-35]	130*	gastritis
[20-35]	130*	gastritis
[40-55]	131*	pneumonia
[40-55]	131*	diabetes
[40-55]	131*	pneumonia
[60-70]	130*	Alzheimer
[60-70]	130*	flu
[60-70]	130*	Alzheimer

(b) 3-anonymous data

age	zipcode	disease
[20-60]	13*	gastritis
[20-60]	13*	pneumonia
[20-60]	13*12	Alzheimer
[25-70]	130*	gastritis
[25-70]	130*	flu
[25-70]	130*	Alzheimer
[35-55]	13*	gastritis
[35-55]	13*	diabetes
[35-55]	13*	pneumonia

(c) 3-diverse data

Figure 6.13: Original and published microdata.

effect of generalization, while making sure that the privacy constraints are satisfied. Therefore, data anonymization is an optimization problem: for all possible data generalizations that satisfy the privacy constraints (k-anonymity or l-diversity), choose the one that minimizes the information loss.

The information loss of a generalized record can be quantified by the number of values in the generalized ranges of its attributes. For example, by generalizing record (35, 13024, gastritis) to ([20-35], 130*, gastritis), we replace the precise combination (35, 13024) by all combinations of ages and zipcodes included in the generalized range ([20-35], 130*). Therefore, the information loss for this record equals to the number of these combinations. By summing up the information losses for all records, we come up with the information loss for the whole published table.

You may wonder how the data anonymization problem is related to spatial data management. In fact, there is a striking similarity between this problem and the problems of clustering and indexing spatial data. Anonymization methods divide the records into groups and replace their values by the generalized values that enclose all exact QID values. Note that every record can be thought of as a point in the multidimensional QID domain. Therefore, the problem of defining the groups is similar to the problem of grouping multidimensional points. The objective of anonymization is to minimize the information loss; this is equivalent to dividing a set of points into groups, such that the MBRs of the groups are minimized. Figure 6.14 illustrates this equivalence. The records from Figure 6.13a are modeled as points in the (age, zipcode) space. The figure shows the best way to divide these points into groups, such that each group has at least 3 points and the areas of their MBRs are minimized. The projections of the MBRs at each dimension define the corresponding generalization ranges for the QIDs of each group.

Therefore, algorithms for spatial data clustering can be used to anonymize microdata. What is more interesting is that the R–tree construction algorithms can be applied for k-anonymization. Recall that the R–tree requires that each leaf node contains at least m and at most M objects, where M is the maximum page capacity. In addition, an important observation is that, for k-anonymity, the anonymized groups should have between k and $2k - 1$ records (a group of $2k$ records or more can trivially be divided into two or more groups of at least k records each). Therefore, by using R–tree construction algorithms with $m = k$, we can construct an R–tree for the microdata and then define

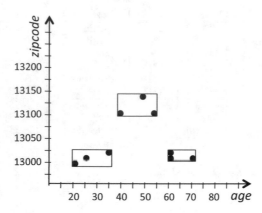

Figure 6.14: Anonymization as spatial clustering.

one anonymization group for each leaf node of the tree. Because the R–tree construction algorithms aim at minimizing the extents of the intermediate entries (i.e., the MBRs of groups), we can achieve generalized data of high quality (i.e., low information loss). An alternative approach to R–tree construction, for data anonymization, would be to spatially sort the data using a space-filling curve and to access the points in this order, while packing them into k-anonymous or l-diverse groups. Spatial histogram construction techniques can also be used as a module for data anonymization.

The concept of k-anonymity can also applied in the context of protecting user identities in location-based service applications. Consider a user who wants to apply a spatial query (e.g., nearest neighbor retrieval), but does not desire to unveil his exact location to the service that answers the query. The reason is that some locations (e.g., home) can directly be linked to the identities of the users. To prevent a server from directly finding out the location of a user, one idea is to *generalize* the user's location to a region (e.g., an MBR), which contains the locations of at least $k - 1$ other users; this way, the server will not be able to identify the user that poses the query inside a group of k users. Since the query location is no longer accurate, the server may return a superset of the exact answer (e.g., the union of nearest neighbors of all points inside the generalized region) and the user in this case has to refine the result using her exact location. In order for the user to determine the generalized region that will be used for her query, an intermediate trusted service could be used, or the users may form trusted groups and use the MBRs of the locations in the groups as queries.

6.6   SPATIAL INFORMATION RETRIEVAL

Standard document search engines support keyword search efficiently. The user provides a set of keywords and the engine finds the most relevant documents to these keywords. The most common query type for keyword search is the *containment* query. Given a set of keywords q, the objective is to find the documents that contain all these keywords.

6.6.1   THE INVERTED FILE

A standard indexing approach for text employed by the majority of search engines is the *inverted file*. It is based on an idea that is indicated by its name, *inversion*. $\mathcal{D}$ is a set of documents, each of which contains a set of terms. The inverted file $I(\mathcal{D})$ for $\mathcal{D}$ is a set of *inverted lists*, one for each term in $\mathcal{A}$. The list that corresponds to term $t \in \mathcal{A}$ contains the document-ids that contain t. Figure 6.15 shows an exemplary inverted file for a set of index terms $\mathcal{A} = \{ace, ant, art, \ldots, zebra\}$. The index is hierarchically divided in two parts; the *directory*, which is an array containing the terms, and the inverted lists.

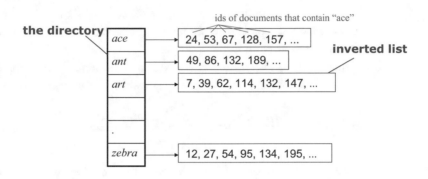

Figure 6.15: An inverted file.

We can use the inverted file to process a containment query q, as follows. For each term $t \in q$, we fetch the corresponding inverted list I_t. The intersection $\bigcap_{t \in q} I_t$ is the query result; since the inverted list of term t contains the ids of all documents that contain t, the intersection of all lists that correspond to the terms of q is the set of documents that contain *all* terms of the query. For example, if we want to find the documents that contain both *ant* and *art*, using the inverted file of Figure 6.15, we just have to join the two lists pointed by the two terms. This intersection will give us document with id=132.

The inverted lists are stored sorted; thus, their intersection can be computed very fast. The computation of a containment query requires accessing and merging as many lists as the number of terms in the query. The directory entries can also be indexed, in order to find the lists that correspond to a containment query, efficiently. This can be achieved with the help of a hash index or even a B^+–tree. For efficient accessing and intersection of the lists, their contents are usually stored in continuous disk segments (or even separate files). The fact that the lists are ordered by document-id also enables the application of effective compression techniques (e.g., run-length encoding) that significantly reduce the index size.

6.6.2   RANKING BY RELEVANCE

The result of a containment query might be too large and overwhelming for the user. In addition, queries with too many keywords may contain very few or no results. *Ranking* queries are an alternative to containment queries, which perform search in a more flexible way and also rank the documents based on their relevance to the keywords, according to some *relevance* measure. The *vector* model is used for documents; instead of simply modeling a document by the set of words it contains, each document D is represented by an r-dimensional *weights* vector $\vec{w}_D = \{w_{1,D}, w_{2,D}, \ldots, w_{r,D}\}$, where $r = |\mathcal{A}|$ is the total number of terms in the system. The weights are non-negative. A set of query terms can also be converted to a weights vector $\vec{q}$, based on the terms it contains; for each term t contained in the query the corresponding weight q_t is set to 1, while for all other terms the weights are set to 0. The user may also opt to give higher weight to some of the query terms. Now, instead of finding the documents that contain the query terms, we can *rank* the documents based on their relevance to the query terms. The similarity between a document D and a query q can be quantified by the *cosine* and *angle* between the corresponding weights vectors $\vec{w}_D$ and $\vec{q}$:

$$sim(d, q) = \frac{\vec{w}_D \bullet \vec{q}}{|\vec{w}_D| \times |\vec{q}|} = \frac{\sum_{i=1}^{r} w_{i,D} \times q_i}{\sqrt{\sum_{i=1}^{r} w_{i,D}^2} \times \sqrt{\sum_{i=1}^{r} q_i^2}} \tag{6.3}$$

Here $|\vec{x}|$ denotes the norm of vector $\vec{x}$. In the denominator, $|\vec{q}|$ does not affect the relative ordering of documents, since it is the same for all of them. The factor $|\vec{w}_D|$ is used for normalization of the similarity score. Since all $w_{i,D}$'s and q_i's are non-negative, $sim(D, q)$ ranges from 0 to 1. Note that with this model a document's similarity score can be positive even if it does not contain all query terms.

It remains to discuss how the weightings of the terms in a document can be defined. How do we assign a weight to a term t that is contained in a document D? A practical weighting scheme works as follows. First, we define the *normalized frequency* $f_{t,D}$ of t as follows:

$$f_{t,D} = \frac{count(t, D)}{\max_{x \in \mathcal{A}} count(x, D)} \tag{6.4}$$

where $count(t, D)$ is the number of times t appears in document D. The denominator is used to normalize the importance of t in D by dividing it with frequency of the term having the maximum number of occurrences in D. The weight of t in D is now defined as follows:

$$w_{t,D} = f_{t,D} \times \log \frac{|\mathcal{D}|}{|\mathcal{D}_t|} \tag{6.5}$$

The right factor of the equation corresponds to the *inverse document frequency* of term t, which is defined by the logarithm of the ratio: the number of documents $|\mathcal{D}|$ in the collection over the number $|\mathcal{D}_t|$ of documents that contain t.

Apart from weighing terms for measuring similarity, other models are also being used. A popular measure (PageRank) for web pages, used by Google, defines relevance using hyperlinks. A web page is considered relevant if it contains the desired search words and in addition it is *popular*. Popularity is assessed by the number of hyperlinks from other pages that point to the document. By combining weighted vector similarity with popularity, we can get an effective measure for the relevance of a document to a set of query terms.

6.6.3 INDEXING FOR RANKING QUERIES

A nice feature of the inverted file is that it can be used to evaluate ranking queries, as well as containment queries, as we saw before. For ranking queries, we adapt the structure of the inverted lists to contain not only document-ids but also weights. For instance, the inverted list for term t contains all documents that contain the term. Together with the id of each such document, we store $w_{t,D}$ in the corresponding list entry. Note that $w_{t,D}$ should be positive; otherwise, t is not contained in D.

Evaluation of a ranking query can now be performed as follows. Like before, we access the inverted lists attached to the index terms of the query. Unlike before, we do not compute the intersection of the lists, but we synchronously scan and merge them to find for each document D that contains at least one term of q, the weights of the terms in D. If a document-id does not appear in a list, then the corresponding query term does not appear in the document, thus its weight is 0. As an example, consider the inverted file of Figure 6.16, which is an extension of the structure in Figure 6.15. Assume that we want to retrieve documents relevant to the terms {*ant, art*}, in order of their relevance. The merge algorithm first encounters document-id 7, for which $w_{art,7} = 2$ and $w_{ant,7} = 0$, since 7 does not appear in the list of *ant*. Continuing this way, we access all document-ids D that contain either *ant* or *art*, or both of these terms and measure $sim(D, q)$, using Equation 6.3. Finally, we sort the documents based on their similarity to q and return the result. Note that a relevant document must appear in the list of *ant* or *art*; document-ids (e.g., 1) that do not appear in some of the lists will have weight 0 at all query terms, so their similarity to q is 0 based on Equation 6.3.

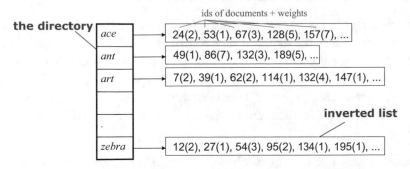

Figure 6.16: Using the inverted file for ranking queries.

6.6.4   SPATIAL KEYWORD SEARCH

Documents often carry spatial features. For example, a webpage may explicitly include a spatial location (e.g., address in the webpage of a person or organization), or the text included in the document may refer to locations at various granularity levels (e.g., there may be a discussion about a country). The locations associated to a document are not essentially explicit (e.g., "a city near Barcelona" is an implicit location) and the document is not essentially physically hosted to the location(s) it refers to.

As already discussed, the result of a keyword search may be overwhelmingly large. Naturally, new methods to filter or rank query result should be used to make it more informative. The spatial features of documents offer such a possibility. Queries can be enriched to include not only a set of keywords, but also a spatial region. Such queries are especially useful in location-based services where mobile users are interested in information related to their location. For example, a spatial keyword query could be "find all documents about vegetarian food within 100m from my current location". This query has a textual component (vegetarian food) and a spatial search component. The result is the set of documents which include the search keywords and also refer to places within the spatial range.

In order to support spatial keyword search, search engines extract and encode spatial information for each document. Based on the textual content of the document (e.g., geographic terms, zipcodes, telephone area codes), a *spatial footprint*, containing the set of locations associated with the document is computed. To evaluate a spatial keyword query, the engine can follow one of the following approaches:

- **Text-first search** As in classic, keyword search, an inverted file is used to find the documents that contain the keywords of the query. For each qualifying document, its spatial footprint is retrieved and compared against the spatial predicate of the query; documents satisfy it are output. This approach is expected to be efficient if the textual part of the query is very selective (there are very few documents that include the keywords).

- **Geo-first search** The spatial footprints of documents are indexed using a spatial access method (e.g., an R–tree). Since the footprint may contain different locations that could be far from each other, a document may be represented by multiple spatial regions in the index. The spatial index is used to find the documents that qualify the spatial predicate of the query. For each document, we then check whether it contains the query keywords. This approach is expected to be efficient for queries where the spatial predicate is very selective, but the textual part is not.

- **Combined search** The best approach, in the general case, would be to simultaneously use both the textual and spatial components of the query to locate the qualifying documents efficiently. Several indexing approaches have been proposed in this direction. An interesting approach is to assign identifiers to documents based on their spatial footprints. The documents are spatially ordered, using a space-filling curve, and take their IDs from this order. Given a spatial keyword query, the inverted lists corresponding to the keywords are accessed, as in keyword-only search; however, the spatial predicate of the query *excludes* the intervals in the inverted lists that are irrelevant to it. This way, only document ids that qualify the spatial predicate are accessed and processed. For example, consider the inverted file in Figure 6.17, where documents are tagged with locations on the map shown on the right of the figure and a space-filling curve assigns ids to them (e.g., the spatial footprint of the document with id=4 is the point with Z-order 4). A spatial keyword query with keywords {*ant, art*} and spatial range *W* (denoted by the dashed rectangle in the figure) would be processed by accessing only the shaded parts of the two inverted lists for *ant* and *art*, since only these intervals can include document-ids that are inside the query range. Alternative indexing methods for combined spatial and keyword search extend the R–tree to support keyword-based retrieval. One idea is to store document-ids at the leaf nodes of the R–tree (which indexes the documents based on their spatial footprints) and augment each entry of the R–tree with a *signature* which summarizes the set of keywords contained in the documents of the sub-tree pointed by the entry. Subtrees can then be filtered not only based on spatial predicates but also if they do not contain some of the query keywords. Another idea is to link the R–tree nodes with inverted files containing inverted lists only for the keywords included in the corresponding subtree. These R–tree extensions are mostly appropriate for objects (i.e., documents, tagged-images, etc.) which contain only a small number of keywords from a limited dictionary.

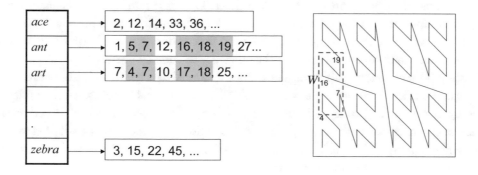

Figure 6.17: Spatial keyword search using the inverted file and document-ids based on Z-order.

6.7   SUMMARY

There is a wide range of research fields that benefit from spatial data management technology. Spatial access methods and search techniques have been extended for the effective management of large-scale moving objects databases. In addition to managing historical spatio-temporal data, methods for predicting and searching the future locations of moving objects have been proposed. The time dimension introduces new and challenging query types, including snapshot queries, time-interval queries, continuous queries, and time-parameterized queries.

In many applications, objects are abstracted and modeled as high dimensional points. Distance metrics are then used to model dissimilarity between the objects. Therefore, similarity search in content-based retrieval and data mining applications can be modeled by range or nearest neighbor search in a high dimensional space. The curse of dimensionality renders spatial access methods, like the R–tree, ineffective. The GEMINI framework alleviates this issue, by approximating the high dimensional points by low dimensional points and employing lower bounding properties of the low dimensional space to apply indexing and avoid exhaustive search.

Ranking of data objects, based on multiple criteria, is an important module of database systems and search engines. Each ranking criterion defines a total order for the objects. A top-k query merges these total orders using an aggregate function and limits the output to the k objects with the highest aggregate score. The skyline of a dataset with multiple ranking criteria contains the objects that are not dominated by any object in the dataset. Spatial data management techniques facilitate the efficient processing of top-k and skyline queries. If the dataset is indexed by an R–tree, the best-first nearest neighbor search algorithm can be extended to support both these query types.

Main data mining tasks, such as clustering and classification can make use of spatial indexing and search to improve efficiency. Nearest neighbor search is a common module of clustering and classification algorithms; this module is implemented efficiently with the help of spatial indexing. Some data mining concepts, such as spatial collocations, apply on spatial data. Finally, OLAP operations can benefit from multi-dimensional indexes. The aggregate R–tree is an extension of the R–tree, which supports range aggregate queries. Besides indexing the fact table of a data warehouse in order to facilitate aggregate range selections on different dimensional attributes, spatial access methods can index data cubes and improve the efficiency of cube by operations.

Privacy-preserving data publishing generalizes relational data before publishing them, in order to prevent adversaries from linking sensitive information with real persons. k-anonymity and l-diversity are two popular privacy models. The problem of data generalization is very similar to spatial access construction. For example, R–tree construction algorithms can be adapted to solve the data anonymization problem. Finally, location anonymity is a privacy model aiming at the protection of user identities in location-based services.

The inverted file is a standard indexing method in Information Retrieval, used to accelerate keyword containment and keyword similarity queries over document collections. Documents often carry spatial features. Spatial keyword search asks for documents that contain (or are similar to) a set of keywords and they refer to information close to a query location. Advanced indexing approaches extend either the inverted file to support spatial search or the R–tree to support keyword search.

BIBLIOGRAPHIC NOTES

The problem of modeling and querying moving objects is formally studied by Güting et al. [2000]. An earlier model was by proposed by Sistla et al. [1997]. The textbook by Güting and Schneider

[2005] is a comprehensive coverage of the models and technology behind moving object databases. SECONDO [Güting et al., 2005] is a spatio-temporal database system prototype.

Tao et al. [2004a] proposed a model for predicting the future movement of objects based on their current and past locations. Mokbel et al. [2004] was one of the first works to study the problem of continuously evaluating queries in moving object databases. Time-parameterized queries were introduced and studied by Tao and Papadias [2002]. Using safe regions to continuously monitor the results of spatial queries over moving objects was suggested by Hu et al. [2005].

3D R–trees and TB–trees for indexing past object trajectories were proposed by Pfoser et al. [2000]. The MV3R–tree [Tao and Papadias, 2001] is a hybrid index that combines the structures of the multi-version (i.e., historical) R–tree [Nascimento and Silva, 1998] and the 3D R–tree. The TPR–tree for indexing future positions of objects was proposed by Saltenis et al. [2000] and later optimized to the TPR*–tree by Tao et al. [2003]. Indexing the future positions of moving objects in the dual space was theoretically studied by Kollios et al. [1999]. This approach was later implemented and tested [Kollios et al., 2005, Patel et al., 2004]. Other indexes for future object positions that we reviewed in this chapter are the B^x–tree [Jensen et al., 2004] and the B^{dual}–tree [Yiu et al., 2008]. The RUM–tree [Silva et al., 2009] is an update-efficient variant of the R–tree, which can be used for update-intensive spatial data (e.g., positions of moving objects). MOVIES [Dittrich et al., 2011] is another update-efficient indexing approach for moving objects, which continuously bulk-loads short-lived main-memory snapshot indexes and throws them away after their expiration. Predictive indexes for moving objects were experimentally compared by Chen et al. [2008].

Image transformation and indexing based on color histograms is discussed by Swain and Ballard [1991]. The ineffectiveness of spatial access methods in high dimensional spaces was studied analytically and experimentally by Beyer et al. [1999] and Weber et al. [1998], respectively. Specialized indexes and storage for nearest neighbor search in high dimensional data were proposed by Berchtold et al. [1996] (the X–tree), Weber et al. [1998] (VA–file), Sakurai et al. [2000] (the A–tree), Yu et al. [2001] (iDistance), de Vries et al. [2002] (BOND).

The GEMINI approach was developed by Christos Faloutsos, initially for subsequence matching [Faloutsos et al., 1994] and then for multimedia indexing by Faloutsos and Lin [1995] and Korn et al. [1996]. FastMap [Faloutsos and Lin, 1995], in particular, is an elegant and powerful method for dimensionality reduction, which can be used when only distance graphs are available for the searched objects in the primary space (but not absolute coordinates). Korn et al. [1996] elaborate on the two-step similarity range and ranking retrieval, for complex distance functions in the primary (high-dimensional) space. Later, Seidl and Kriegel [1998] showed how to improve the two-step ranking algorithm to the muli-step algorithm, which avoids unnecessary distance computations in the primary space, by applying incremental nearest neighbor search [Hjaltason and Samet, 1999] in the indexed space.

Evaluation techniques for multi-criteria top-k queries are surveyed by a recent article [Ilyas et al., 2008]. Classic approaches for this problem that do not rely on indexing were proposed and analyzed by Fagin [1998]. The geometric approach that indexes the data using an R–tree and applies best-first search to solve the problem is proposed by Tao et al. [2007]. The skyline operator was introduced to the database community by Börzsönyi et al. [2001] and the best-first evaluation techniques over R–trees was proposed by Papadias et al. [2005a]. Aggregate nearest neighbor queries in spatial databases are studied in Papadias et al. [2005b]. The spatial skyline query was introduced in Sharifzadeh and Shahabi [2006].

There are several data mining textbooks [Han et al., 2011, Tan et al., 2005], which describe the dominant mining tasks and methods. Issues and trends in spatial data mining have been discussed in Shekhar's book [Shekhar and Chawla, 2003]. The term on-line analytical processing (OLAP) was coined by Edgar F. Codd in a white paper [Codd et al., 1993]. The CUBE BY operator was introduced by Gray et al. [1996]. The use of R–trees to index and maintain a data cube in order to evaluate OLAP queries efficiently was proposed by Roussopoulos et al. [1997]. The idea of augmenting aggregate information in R–trees in order to efficiently process range aggregate and OLAP queries at arbitrary spatial granulation levels was explored by Lazaridis and Mehrotra [2001] and Papadias et al. [2001].

The k-anonymity [Samarati, 2001, Sweeney, 2002] and l-diversity [Machanavajjhala et al., 2006] models have been proposed to warrant user privacy in microdata publishing. Iwuchukwu and Naughton [2007] model k-anonymization as a spatial indexing problem and show how spatial database technology can help towards scalable and incremental anonymization. In a similar direction, Ghinita et al. [2009] showed how space-filling curves can be used to order and pack the data into anonymized groups. User anonymity in location-based applications has been studied by Mokbel et al. [2006] and Ghinita et al. [2007]. An overview of privacy-preserving data publishing techniques is offered by Wong and Fu [2010].

Textbooks in information retrieval [Baeza-Yates and Ribeiro-Neto, 2011, Manning et al., 2008] describe in-depth models and indexes for text retrieval. Chen et al. [2006] propose a framework for extracting spatial features from web documents as spatial fingerprints and indexing them for efficient spatial keyword search. The prevailing indexing method in their study orders the fingerprints using a space-filling curve and assigns ids to documents based on the order on their documents on the curve. The documents are then indexed by means of inverted files. For a spatial keyword query, only intervals on the inverted lists that qualify the spatial predicate of the query have to be accessed. Extensions of the R–tree that index the keywords describing the spatial objects and support spatial keyword search are proposed by Felipe et al. [2008] and Cong et al. [2009].

Bibliography

Ashraf Aboulnaga and Jeffrey F. Naughton. Accurate estimation of the cost of spatial selections. In *Proc. 16th Int. Conf. on Data Engineering*, pages 123–134, 2000. DOI: 10.1109/ICDE.2000.839399 Cited on page(s) 64

Ittai Abraham, Amos Fiat, Andrew V. Goldberg, and Renato Fonseca F. Werneck. Highway dimension, shortest paths, and provably efficient algorithms. In *Proc. 21th Annual ACM-SIAM Symp. on Discrete Algorithms*, pages 782–793, 2010. Cited on page(s) 82

Swarup Acharya, Viswanath Poosala, and Sridhar Ramaswamy. Selectivity estimation in spatial databases. In *Proc. ACM SIGMOD Int. Conf. on Management of Data*, pages 13–24, 1999. DOI: 10.1145/304181.304184 Cited on page(s) 64

Rakesh Agrawal and H. V. Jagadish. Materialization and incremental update of path information. In *Proc. 5th Int. Conf. on Data Engineering*, pages 374–383, 1989. Cited on page(s) 82

Rakesh Agrawal and H. V. Jagadish. Algorithms for searching massive graphs. *IEEE Trans. Knowl. and Data Eng.*, 6(2):225–238, 1994. DOI: 10.1109/69.277767 Cited on page(s) 82

Ning An, Ji Jin, and Anand Sivasubramaniam. Toward an accurate analysis of range queries on spatial data. *IEEE Trans. Knowl. and Data Eng.*, 15(2):305–323, 2003. DOI: 10.1109/TKDE.2003.1185836 Cited on page(s) 64

Lars Arge, Octavian Procopiuc, Sridhar Ramaswamy, Torsten Suel, and Jeffrey Scott Vitter. Scalable sweeping-based spatial join. In *Proc. 24th Int. Conf. on Very Large Data Bases*, pages 570–581, 1998. Cited on page(s) 63

Lars Arge, Octavian Procopiuc, Sridhar Ramaswamy, Torsten Suel, Jan Vahrenhold, and Jeffrey Scott Vitter. A unified approach for indexed and non-indexed spatial joins. In *Advances in Database Technology, Proc. 7th Int. Conf. on Extending Database Technology*, pages 413–429, 2000. Cited on page(s) 63

Lars Arge, Mark de Berg, Herman J. Haverkort, and Ke Yi. The priority r-tree: A practically efficient and worst-case optimal r-tree. In *Proc. ACM SIGMOD Int. Conf. on Management of Data*, pages 347–358, 2004. DOI: 10.1145/1007568.1007608 Cited on page(s) 33

Ricardo A. Baeza-Yates and Berthier A. Ribeiro-Neto. *Modern Information Retrieval - the concepts and technology behind search*. Addison-Wesley, 2011. Cited on page(s) 118

Holger Bast, Stefan Funke, Domagoj Matijevic, Peter Sanders, and Dominik Schultes. In transit to constant time shortest-path queries in road networks. In *Proc. Workshop on Algorithm Engineering and Experiments*, 2007. Cited on page(s) 82

Ludger Becker, Klaus Hinrichs, and Ulrich Finke. A new algorithm for computing joins with grid files. In *Proc. 9th Int. Conf. on Data Engineering*, pages 190–197, 1993. DOI: 10.1109/ICDE.1993.344063 Cited on page(s) 63

Norbert Beckmann and Bernhard Seeger. A revised R*-tree in comparison with related index structures. In *Proc. ACM SIGMOD Int. Conf. on Management of Data*, pages 799–812, 2009. Cited on page(s) 33

Norbert Beckmann, Hans-Peter Kriegel, Ralf Schneider, and Bernhard Seeger. The R*-tree: An efficient and robust access method for points and rectangles. In *Proc. ACM SIGMOD Int. Conf. on Management of Data*, pages 322–331, 1990. DOI: 10.1145/93605.98741 Cited on page(s) 33

Alberto Belussi and Christos Faloutsos. Estimating the selectivity of spatial queries using the 'correlation' fractal dimension. In *Proc. 21th Int. Conf. on Very Large Data Bases*, pages 299–310, 1995. Cited on page(s) 64

Stefan Berchtold, Daniel A. Keim, and Hans-Peter Kriegel. The X-tree : An index structure for high-dimensional data. In *Proc. 22th Int. Conf. on Very Large Data Bases*, pages 28–39, 1996. Cited on page(s) 117

Kevin S. Beyer, Jonathan Goldstein, Raghu Ramakrishnan, and Uri Shaft. When is "nearest neighbor" meaningful? In *Proc. 7th Int. Conf. on Database Theory*, pages 217–235, 1999. Cited on page(s) 117

Christian Böhm, Bernhard Braunmüller, Florian Krebs, and Hans-Peter Kriegel. Epsilon grid order: An algorithm for the similarity join on massive high-dimensional data. In *Proc. ACM SIGMOD Int. Conf. on Management of Data*, pages 379–388, 2001. Cited on page(s) 64

Karla A. V. Borges, Clodoveu A. Davis, and Alberto H. F. Laender. OMT-G: An object-oriented data model for geographic applications. *GeoInformatica*, 5(3):221–260, 2001. DOI: 10.1023/A:1011482030093 Cited on page(s) 18

Stephan Börzsönyi, Donald Kossmann, and Konrad Stocker. The skyline operator. In *Proc. 17th Int. Conf. on Data Engineering*, pages 421–430, 2001. DOI: 10.1109/ICDE.2001.914855 Cited on page(s) 118

Thomas Brinkhoff, Hans-Peter Kriegel, and Bernhard Seeger. Efficient processing of spatial joins using R-trees. In *Proc. ACM SIGMOD Int. Conf. on Management of Data*, pages 237–246, 1993. DOI: 10.1145/170036.170075 Cited on page(s) 63

Thomas Brinkhoff, Hans-Peter Kriegel, Ralf Schneider, and Bernhard Seeger. Multi-step processing of spatial joins. In *Proc. ACM SIGMOD Int. Conf. on Management of Data*, pages 197–208, 1994. DOI: 10.1145/191843.191880 Cited on page(s) 63

Su Chen, Christian S. Jensen, and Dan Lin. A benchmark for evaluating moving object indexes. *Proceedings of the VLDB Endowment*, 1(2):1574–1585, 2008. Cited on page(s) 117

Tao Chen, Markus Schneider, Ganesh Viswanathan, and Wenjie Yuan. The objects interaction matrix for modeling cardinal directions in spatial databases. In *Proc. 15th Int. Conf. on Database Systems for Advanced Applications*, pages 218–232, 2010. DOI: 10.1007/978-3-642-12026-8_18 Cited on page(s) 18

Yen-Yu Chen, Torsten Suel, and Alexander Markowetz. Efficient query processing in geographic web search engines. In *Proc. ACM SIGMOD Int. Conf. on Management of Data*, pages 277–288, 2006. DOI: 10.1145/1142473.1142505 Cited on page(s) 118

Edgar F. Codd, Sally B. Codd, and Clynch T. Salley. *Providing OLAP (On-line Analytical Processing) to User-Analysts: An IT Mandate*. Codd & Date, Inc, 1993. Cited on page(s) 118

Gao Cong, Christian S. Jensen, and Dingming Wu. Efficient retrieval of the top-k most relevant spatial web objects. *Proceedings of the VLDB Endowment*, 2(1):337–348, 2009. Cited on page(s) 118

Antonio Corral, Yannis Manolopoulos, Yannis Theodoridis, and Michael Vassilakopoulos. Closest pair queries in spatial databases. In *Proc. ACM SIGMOD Int. Conf. on Management of Data*, pages 189–200, 2000. DOI: 10.1145/342009.335414 Cited on page(s) 64

Mark de Berg, Otfried Cheong, Marc van Kreveld, and Mark Overmars. *Computational Geometry: Algorithms and Applications*. Springer-Verlag, 2008. Cited on page(s) 32

Juliano Lopes de Oliveira, Fatima Pires, and Claudia Bauzer Medeiros. An environment for modeling and design of geographic applications. *GeoInformatica*, 1(1):29–58, 1997. DOI: 10.1023/A:1009704100446 Cited on page(s) 18

Arjen P. de Vries, Nikos Mamoulis, Niels Nes, and Martin L. Kersten. Efficient k-NN search on vertically decomposed data. In *Proc. ACM SIGMOD Int. Conf. on Management of Data*, pages 322–333, 2002. Cited on page(s) 117

Edsger W. Dijkstra. A note on two problems in connexion with graphs. *Numerische Mathematik*, 1: 269–271, 1959. DOI: 10.1007/BF01386390 Cited on page(s) 82

Jens Dittrich, Lukas Blunschi, and Marcos Antonio Vaz Salles. MOVIES: indexing moving objects by shooting index images. *GeoInformatica*, 15(4):727–767, 2011. DOI: 10.1007/s10707-011-0122-y Cited on page(s) 117

Max J. Egenhofer. Reasoning about binary topological relations. In *Proc. 2nd Int. Symp. Advances in Spatial Databases*, pages 143–160, 1991. Cited on page(s) 18

Max J. Egenhofer, Eliseo Clementini, and Paolino Di Felice. Topological relations between regions with holes. *International Journal of Geographical Information Systems*, 8(2):129–142, 1994. DOI: 10.1080/02693799408901990 Cited on page(s) 18

Ronald Fagin. Fuzzy queries in multimedia database systems. In *Proc. 17th ACM SIGACT-SIGMOD-SIGART Symp. on Principles of Database Systems*, pages 1–10, 1998. Cited on page(s) 117

Christos Faloutsos and King-Ip Lin. Fastmap: A fast algorithm for indexing, data-mining and visualization of traditional and multimedia datasets. In *Proc. ACM SIGMOD Int. Conf. on Management of Data*, pages 163–174, 1995. Cited on page(s) 117

Christos Faloutsos, M. Ranganathan, and Yannis Manolopoulos. Fast subsequence matching in time-series databases. In *Proc. ACM SIGMOD Int. Conf. on Management of Data*, pages 419–429, 1994. DOI: 10.1145/191843.191925 Cited on page(s) 117

Christos Faloutsos, Bernhard Seeger, Agma J. M. Traina, and Caetano Traina Jr. Spatial join selectivity using power laws. In *Proc. ACM SIGMOD Int. Conf. on Management of Data*, pages 177–188, 2000. DOI: 10.1145/342009.335412 Cited on page(s) 64

Ian De Felipe, Vagelis Hristidis, and Naphtali Rishe. Keyword search on spatial databases. In *Proc. 24th Int. Conf. on Data Engineering*, pages 656–665, 2008. Cited on page(s) 118

Raphael A. Finkel and Jon Louis Bentley. Quad trees: A data structure for retrieval on composite keys. *Acta Informatica*, 4:1–9, 1974. DOI: 10.1007/BF00288933 Cited on page(s) 32

Andrew U. Frank. Application of DBMS to land information systems. In *Proc. 7th Int. Conf. on Very Data Bases*, pages 448–453, 1981. Cited on page(s) 19

Christian Freksa. Using orientation information for qualitative spatial reasoning. In *Proc. Int. GIS Conference on Theories and Methods of Spatio-Temporal Reasoning in Geographic Space*, pages 162–178, 1992. Cited on page(s) 18

Volker Gaede and Oliver Günther. Multidimensional access methods. *ACM Comput. Surv.*, 30(2): 170–231, 1998. DOI: 10.1145/280277.280279 Cited on page(s) 18, 32

Gabriel Ghinita, Panos Kalnis, and Spiros Skiadopoulos. Prive: anonymous location-based queries in distributed mobile systems. In *WWW*, pages 371–380, 2007. Cited on page(s) 118

Gabriel Ghinita, Panagiotis Karras, Panos Kalnis, and Nikos Mamoulis. A framework for efficient data anonymization under privacy and accuracy constraints. *ACM Trans. Database Syst.*, 34(2), 2009. DOI: 10.1145/1538909.1538911 Cited on page(s) 118

Andrew V. Goldberg and Chris Harrelson. Computing the shortest path: search meets graph theory. In *Proc. 16th Annual ACM-SIAM Symp. on Discrete Algorithms*, pages 156–165, 2005. Cited on page(s) 82

Andrew V. Goldberg, Haim Kaplan, and Renato Fonseca F. Werneck. Reach for A*: Shortest path algorithms with preprocessing. In *Proc. Workshop on Algorithm Engineering and Experiments*, pages 129–143, 2006. Cited on page(s) 82

Jim Gray, Adam Bosworth, Andrew Layman, and Hamid Pirahesh. Data cube: A relational aggregation operator generalizing group-by, cross-tab, and sub-total. In *Proc. 12th Int. Conf. on Data Engineering*, pages 152–159, 1996. Cited on page(s) 118

Ralf Hartmut Güting. An introduction to spatial database systems. *VLDB J.*, 3(4):357–399, 1994. DOI: 10.1007/BF01231601 Cited on page(s) 9, 18

Ralf Hartmut Güting and Markus Schneider. *Moving Objects Databases*. Morgan Kaufmann, 2005. Cited on page(s) 116

Ralf Hartmut Güting, Michael H. Böhlen, Martin Erwig, Christian S. Jensen, Nikos A. Lorentzos, Markus Schneider, and Michalis Vazirgiannis. A foundation for representing and querying moving objects. *ACM Trans. Database Syst.*, 25(1):1–42, 2000. DOI: 10.1145/352958.352963 Cited on page(s) 116

Ralf Hartmut Güting, Victor Teixeira de Almeida, Dirk Ansorge, Thomas Behr, Zhiming Ding, Thomas Höse, Frank Hoffmann, Markus Spiekermann, and Ulrich Telle. Secondo: An extensible dbms platform for research prototyping and teaching. In *Proc. 21st Int. Conf. on Data Engineering*, pages 1115–1116, 2005. Cited on page(s) 9, 117

Ronald J. Gutman. Reach-based routing: A new approach to shortest path algorithms optimized for road networks. In *Proc. Workshop on Algorithm Engineering and Experiments*, pages 100–111, 2004. Cited on page(s) 82

Antonin Guttman. R-trees: A dynamic index structure for spatial searching. In *Proc. ACM SIGMOD Int. Conf. on Management of Data*, pages 47–57, 1984. DOI: 10.1145/971697.602266 Cited on page(s) 33

Marios Hadjieleftheriou, Erik G. Hoel, and Vassilis J. Tsotras. Sail: A spatial index library for efficient application integration. *GeoInformatica*, 9(4):367–389, 2005. DOI: 10.1007/s10707-005-4577-6 Cited on page(s) 33

Jiawei Han, Micheline Kamber, and Jian Pei. *Data Mining: Concepts and Techniques*. Morgan Kaufmann, 2011. Cited on page(s) 118

Peter E. Hart, Nils J. Nilsson, and Bertram Raphael. A formal basis for the heuristic determination of minimum cost paths. *IEEE Trans. on Systems Science and Cybernetics*, SSC-4(2):100–107, 1968. DOI: 10.1109/TSSC.1968.300136 Cited on page(s) 82

Gísli R. Hjaltason and Hanan Samet. Incremental distance join algorithms for spatial databases. In *Proc. ACM SIGMOD Int. Conf. on Management of Data*, pages 237–248, 1998. DOI: 10.1145/276305.276326 Cited on page(s) 64

Gísli R. Hjaltason and Hanan Samet. Distance browsing in spatial databases. *ACM Trans. Database Syst.*, 24(2):265–318, 1999. DOI: 10.1145/320248.320255 Cited on page(s) 63, 117

Haibo Hu, Jianliang Xu, and Dik Lun Lee. A generic framework for monitoring continuous spatial queries over moving objects. In *Proc. ACM SIGMOD Int. Conf. on Management of Data*, pages 479–490, 2005. DOI: 10.1145/1066157.1066212 Cited on page(s) 117

Ihab F. Ilyas, George Beskales, and Mohamed A. Soliman. A survey of top- query processing techniques in relational database systems. *ACM Comput. Surv.*, 40(4), 2008. DOI: 10.1145/1391729.1391730 Cited on page(s) 117

Tochukwu Iwuchukwu and Jeffrey F. Naughton. K-anonymization as spatial indexing: Toward scalable and incremental anonymization. In *Proc. 33rd Int. Conf. on Very Large Data Bases*, pages 746–757, 2007. Cited on page(s) 118

Edwin H. Jacox and Hanan Samet. Spatial join techniques. *ACM Trans. Database Syst.*, 32(1):7, 2007. DOI: 10.1145/1206049.1206056 Cited on page(s) 63

Christian S. Jensen, Dan Lin, and Beng Chin Ooi. Query and update efficient b+-tree based indexing of moving objects. In *Proc. 30th Int. Conf. on Very Large Data Bases*, pages 768–779, 2004. Cited on page(s) 117

Ning Jing, Yun-Wu Huang, and Elke A. Rundensteiner. Hierarchical encoded path views for path query processing: An optimal model and its performance evaluation. *IEEE Trans. Knowl. and Data Eng.*, 10(3):409–432, 1998. DOI: 10.1109/69.687976 Cited on page(s) 82

Sungwon Jung and Sakti Pramanik. An efficient path computation model for hierarchically structured topographical road maps. *IEEE Trans. Knowl. and Data Eng.*, 14(5):1029–1046, 2002. DOI: 10.1109/TKDE.2002.1033772 Cited on page(s) 82

Ibrahim Kamel and Christos Faloutsos. On packing R-trees. In *Proc. Int. Conf. on Information and Knowledge Management*, pages 490–499, 1993. Cited on page(s) 33

Ibrahim Kamel and Christos Faloutsos. Hilbert R-tree: An improved R-tree using fractals. In *Proc. 20th Int. Conf. on Very Large Data Bases*, pages 500–509, 1994. Cited on page(s) 33

George Kollios, Dimitrios Gunopulos, and Vassilis J. Tsotras. On indexing mobile objects. In *Proc. 18th ACM SIGACT-SIGMOD-SIGART Symp. on Principles of Database Systems*, pages 261–272, 1999. Cited on page(s) 117

George Kollios, Dimitris Papadopoulos, Dimitrios Gunopulos, and Vassilis J. Tsotras. Indexing mobile objects using dual transformations. *VLDB J.*, 14(2):238–256, 2005. DOI: 10.1007/s00778-004-0139-z Cited on page(s) 117

Flip Korn, Nikolaos Sidiropoulos, Christos Faloutsos, Eliot Siegel, and Zenon Protopapas. Fast nearest neighbor search in medical image databases. In *Proc. 22th Int. Conf. on Very Large Data Bases*, pages 215–226, 1996. Cited on page(s) 117

Nick Koudas and Kenneth C. Sevcik. Size separation spatial join. In *Proc. ACM SIGMOD Int. Conf. on Management of Data*, pages 324–335, 1997. DOI: 10.1145/253262.253340 Cited on page(s) 63

Nick Koudas and Kenneth C. Sevcik. High dimensional similarity joins: Algorithms and performance evaluation. *IEEE Trans. Knowl. and Data Eng.*, 12(1):3–18, 2000. DOI: 10.1109/69.842246 Cited on page(s) 64

Hans-Peter Kriegel, Peer Kröger, Peter Kunath, Matthias Renz, and Tim Schmidt. Proximity queries in large traffic networks. In *Proc. 15th ACM Int. Symp. on Geographic Information Systems*, page 21, 2007. Cited on page(s) 82

Hans-Peter Kriegel, Matthias Renz, and Matthias Schubert. Route skyline queries: A multi-preference path planning approach. In *Proc. 26th Int. Conf. on Data Engineering*, pages 261–272, 2010. Cited on page(s) 83

Robert Laurini and Derek Thompson. *Fundamentals of Spatial Information Systems*. Academic Press, 1992. Cited on page(s) 9, 18

Iosif Lazaridis and Sharad Mehrotra. Progressive approximate aggregate queries with a multi-resolution tree structure. In *Proc. ACM SIGMOD Int. Conf. on Management of Data*, pages 401–412, 2001. DOI: 10.1145/376284.375718 Cited on page(s) 118

Scott T. Leutenegger, J. M. Edgington, and Mario A. Lopez. STR: A simple and efficient algorithm for R-tree packing. In *Proc. 13th Int. Conf. on Data Engineering*, pages 497–506, 1997. DOI: 10.1109/ICDE.1997.582015 Cited on page(s) 33

Gerard Ligozat. Reasoning about cardinal directions. *Journal of Visual Languages and Computing*, 9 (1):23–44, 1998. DOI: 10.1006/jvlc.1997.9999 Cited on page(s) 18

Xuemin Lin, Qing Liu, Yidong Yuan, Xiaofang Zhou, and Hongjun Lu. Summarizing level-two topological relations in large spatial datasets. *ACM Trans. Database Syst.*, 31(2):584–630, 2006. DOI: 10.1145/1138394.1138398 Cited on page(s) 64

Ming-Ling Lo and Chinya V. Ravishankar. Spatial joins using seeded trees. In *Proc. ACM SIGMOD Int. Conf. on Management of Data*, pages 209–220, 1994. DOI: 10.1145/191843.191881 Cited on page(s) 63

Ming-Ling Lo and Chinya V. Ravishankar. Spatial hash-joins. In *Proc. ACM SIGMOD Int. Conf. on Management of Data*, pages 247–258, 1996. DOI: 10.1145/235968.233337 Cited on page(s) 63

Ashwin Machanavajjhala, Johannes Gehrke, Daniel Kifer, and Muthuramakrishnan Venkitasubramaniam. l-diversity: Privacy beyond k-anonymity. In *Proc. 22nd Int. Conf. on Data Engineering*, page 24, 2006. Cited on page(s) 118

Nikos Mamoulis and Dimitris Papadias. Multiway spatial joins. *ACM Trans. Database Syst.*, 26(4): 424–475, 2001a. DOI: 10.1145/503099.503101 Cited on page(s) 63

Nikos Mamoulis and Dimitris Papadias. Selectivity estimation of complex spatial queries. In *Proc. 7th Int. Symp. Advances in Spatial and Temporal Databases*, pages 155–174, 2001b. Cited on page(s) 64

Nikos Mamoulis and Dimitris Papadias. Slot index spatial join. *IEEE Trans. Knowl. and Data Eng.*, 15(1):211–231, 2003. DOI: 10.1109/TKDE.2003.1161591 Cited on page(s) 63

Nikos Mamoulis, Yannis Theodoridis, and Dimitris Papadias. Spatial joins: Algorithms, cost models and optimization techniques. In *Spatial Databases*, pages 155–184. Idea Group, 2005. Cited on page(s) 64

Christopher D. Manning, Prabhakar Raghavan, and Hinrich Schütze. *Introduction to Information Retrieval*. Cambridge University Press, 2008. Cited on page(s) 118

Yannis Manolopoulos, Alexandros Nanopoulos, Apostolos N. Papadopoulos, and Yannis Theodoridis. *R-trees: Theory and Applications*. Springer, 2005. Cited on page(s) 33

Mohamed F. Mokbel, Xiaopeng Xiong, and Walid G. Aref. SINA: Scalable incremental processing of continuous queries in spatio-temporal databases. In *Proc. ACM SIGMOD Int. Conf. on Management of Data*, pages 623–634, 2004. DOI: 10.1145/1007568.1007638 Cited on page(s) 117

Mohamed F. Mokbel, Chi-Yin Chow, and Walid G. Aref. The new Casper: Query processing for location services without compromising privacy. In *Proc. 32nd Int. Conf. on Very Large Data Bases*, pages 763–774, 2006. Cited on page(s) 118

S. Muthukrishnan, Viswanath Poosala, and Torsten Suel. On rectangular partitionings in two dimensions: Algorithms, complexity, and applications. In *Proc. 7th Int. Conf. on Database Theory*, pages 236–256, 1999. Cited on page(s) 64

Mario A. Nascimento and Jefferson R. O. Silva. Towards historical R-trees. In *Proc. 1998 ACM Symp. on Applied Computing*, pages 235–240, 1998. DOI: 10.1145/330560.330692 Cited on page(s) 117

T. A. J. Nicholson. Finding the shortest route between two points in a network. *The Computer Journal*, 9:275–280, 1966. Cited on page(s) 82

Jürg Nievergelt, Hans Hinterberger, and Kenneth C. Sevcik. The grid file: An adaptable, symmetric multikey file structure. *ACM Trans. Database Syst.*, 9(1):38–71, 1984. DOI: 10.1145/348.318586 Cited on page(s) 32

Jack A. Orenstein. Spatial query processing in an object-oriented database system. In *Proc. ACM SIGMOD Int. Conf. on Management of Data*, pages 326–336, 1986. DOI: 10.1145/16856.16886 Cited on page(s) 32

Jack A. Orenstein and Frank Manola. PROBE spatial data modeling and query processing in an image database application. *IEEE Trans. Softw. Eng.*, 14(5):611–629, 1988. DOI: 10.1109/32.6139 Cited on page(s) 19, 32, 63

Dimitris Papadias, Yannis Theodoridis, Timos K. Sellis, and Max J. Egenhofer. Topological relations in the world of minimum bounding rectangles: A study with R-trees. In *Proc. ACM SIGMOD Int. Conf. on Management of Data*, pages 92–103, 1995. DOI: 10.1145/568271.223798 Cited on page(s) 18

Dimitris Papadias, Panos Kalnis, Jun Zhang, and Yufei Tao. Efficient olap operations in spatial data warehouses. In *Proc. 7th Int. Symp. Advances in Spatial and Temporal Databases*, pages 443–459, 2001. Cited on page(s) 118

Dimitris Papadias, Jun Zhang, Nikos Mamoulis, and Yufei Tao. Query processing in spatial network databases. In *Proc. 29th Int. Conf. on Very Large Data Bases*, pages 802–813, 2003. Cited on page(s) 82

Dimitris Papadias, Yufei Tao, Greg Fu, and Bernhard Seeger. Progressive skyline computation in database systems. *ACM Trans. Database Syst.*, 30(1):41–82, 2005a. DOI: 10.1145/1061318.1061320 Cited on page(s) 118

Dimitris Papadias, Yufei Tao, Kyriakos Mouratidis, and Chun Kit Hui. Aggregate nearest neighbor queries in spatial databases. *ACM Trans. Database Syst.*, 30(2):529–576, 2005b. DOI: 10.1145/1071610.1071616 Cited on page(s) 118

Apostolos Papadopoulos, Philippe Rigaux, and Michel Scholl. A performance evaluation of spatial join processing strategies. In *Proc. 6th Int. Symp. Advances in Spatial Databases*, pages 286–307, 1999. DOI: 10.1007/3-540-48482-5_18 Cited on page(s) 63

Jignesh M. Patel and David J. DeWitt. Partition based spatial-merge join. In *Proc. ACM SIGMOD Int. Conf. on Management of Data*, pages 259–270, 1996. DOI: 10.1145/235968.233338 Cited on page(s) 63

Jignesh M. Patel, Yun Chen, and V. Prasad Chakka. STRIPES: An efficient index for predicted trajectories. In *Proc. ACM SIGMOD Int. Conf. on Management of Data*, pages 637–646, 2004. Cited on page(s) 117

Dieter Pfoser, Christian S. Jensen, and Yannis Theodoridis. Novel approaches in query processing for moving object trajectories. In *Proc. 26th Int. Conf. on Very Large Data Bases*, pages 395–406, 2000. Cited on page(s) 117

Franco P. Preparata and Michael Ian Shamos. *Computational Geometry - An Introduction*. Springer, 1985. Cited on page(s) 32

Jochen Renz and Bernhard Nebel. On the complexity of qualitative spatial reasoning: A maximal tractable fragment of the region connection calculus. *Artificial Intelligence*, 108(1-2):69–123, 1999. DOI: 10.1016/S0004-3702(99)00002-8 Cited on page(s) 18

Michael N. Rice and Vassilis J. Tsotras. Graph indexing of road networks for shortest path queries with label restrictions. *Proceedings of the VLDB Endowment*, 4(2):69–80, 2010. Cited on page(s) 83

Philippe Rigaux, Michel Scholl, and Agnès Voisard. *Spatial Databases: With Applications to GIS*. Morgan Kaufmann, 2001. Cited on page(s) 9

John T. Robinson. The k-d-B-tree: A search structure for large multidimensional dynamic indexes. In *Proc. ACM SIGMOD Int. Conf. on Management of Data*, pages 10–18, 1981. Cited on page(s) 33

Doron Rotem. Spatial join indices. In *Proc. 7th Int. Conf. on Data Engineering*, pages 500–509, 1991. Cited on page(s) 63

Nick Roussopoulos and Daniel Leifker. Direct spatial search on pictorial databases using packed R-trees. In *Proc. ACM SIGMOD Int. Conf. on Management of Data*, pages 17–31, 1985. DOI: 10.1145/971699.318900 Cited on page(s) 33

Nick Roussopoulos, Stephen Kelley, and Frédéic Vincent. Nearest neighbor queries. In *Proc. ACM SIGMOD Int. Conf. on Management of Data*, pages 71–79, 1995. DOI: 10.1145/568271.223794 Cited on page(s) 63

Nick Roussopoulos, Yannis Kotidis, and Mema Roussopoulos. Cubetree: Organization of and bulk updates on the data cube. In *Proc. ACM SIGMOD Int. Conf. on Management of Data*, pages 89–99, 1997. DOI: 10.1145/253262.253276 Cited on page(s) 118

Hans Sagan. *Space-Filling Curves*. Springer-Verlag, 1994. Cited on page(s) 32

Yasushi Sakurai, Masatoshi Yoshikawa, Shunsuke Uemura, and Haruhiko Kojima. The A-tree: An index structure for high-dimensional spaces using relative approximation. In *Proc. 26th Int. Conf. on Very Large Data Bases*, pages 516–526, 2000. Cited on page(s) 117

Simonas Saltenis, Christian S. Jensen, Scott T. Leutenegger, and Mario A. Lopez. Indexing the positions of continuously moving objects. In *Proc. ACM SIGMOD Int. Conf. on Management of Data*, pages 331–342, 2000. DOI: 10.1145/342009.335427 Cited on page(s) 117

Pierangela Samarati. Protecting respondents' identities in microdata release. *IEEE Trans. Knowl. and Data Eng.*, 13(6):1010–1027, 2001. DOI: 10.1109/69.971193 Cited on page(s) 118

Hanan Samet. *The Design and Analysis of Spatial Data Structures*. Addison-Wesley, 1990. Cited on page(s) 32

Hanan Samet. *Foundations of Multidimensional and Metric Data Structures*. Morgan Kaufmann, 2006. Cited on page(s) 32, 33

Hanan Samet, Jagan Sankaranarayanan, and Houman Alborzi. Scalable network distance browsing in spatial databases. In *Proc. ACM SIGMOD Int. Conf. on Management of Data*, pages 43–54, 2008. Cited on page(s) 82

Peter Sanders and Dominik Schultes. Highway hierarchies hasten exact shortest path queries. In *Proceedings of European Symposium on Algorithms*, pages 568–579, 2005. Cited on page(s) 82

Jagan Sankaranarayanan and Hanan Samet. Distance oracles for spatial networks. In *Proc. 25th Int. Conf. on Data Engineering*, pages 652–663, 2009. Cited on page(s) 82

Jagan Sankaranarayanan, Houman Alborzi, and Hanan Samet. Efficient query processing on spatial networks. In *Proc. 13th ACM Int. Symp. on Geographic Information Systems*, pages 200–209, 2005. Cited on page(s) 82

Michel Scholl and Agnès Voisard. Thematic map modeling. In *Proc. 1st Int. Symp. Advances in Spatial Databases*, pages 167–190, 1989. Cited on page(s) 18

Thomas Seidl and Hans-Peter Kriegel. Optimal multi-step k-nearest neighbor search. In *Proc. ACM SIGMOD Int. Conf. on Management of Data*, pages 154–165, 1998. DOI: 10.1145/276305.276319 Cited on page(s) 117

Timos K. Sellis, Nick Roussopoulos, and Christos Faloutsos. The R+-tree: A dynamic index for multi-dimensional objects. In *Proc. 13th Int. Conf. on Very Large Data Bases*, pages 507–518, 1987. Cited on page(s) 33

Cyrus Shahabi, Mohammad R. Kolahdouzan, and Mehdi Sharifzadeh. A road network embedding technique for k-nearest neighbor search in moving object databases. *GeoInformatica*, 7(3), 2003. DOI: 10.1023/A:1025153016110 Cited on page(s) 82

Mehdi Sharifzadeh and Cyrus Shahabi. The spatial skyline queries. In *Proc. 32nd Int. Conf. on Very Large Data Bases*, pages 751–762, 2006. Cited on page(s) 118

Shashi Shekhar and Sanjay Chawla. *Spatial Databases: A Tour*. Prentice Hall, 2003. Cited on page(s) 9, 118

Shashi Shekhar and Duen-Ren Liu. Ccam: A connectivity-clustered access method for networks and network computations. *IEEE Trans. Knowl. and Data Eng.*, 9(1):102–119, 1997. DOI: 10.1109/69.567054 Cited on page(s) 82

Shashi Shekhar, Mark Coyle, Brajesh Goyal, Duen-Ren Liu, and Shyamsundar Sarkar. Data models in geographic information systems. *Commun. ACM*, 40(4):103–111, 1997. DOI: 10.1145/248448.248465 Cited on page(s) 18

Shashi Shekhar, Sanjay Chawla, Sivakumar Ravada, Andrew Fetterer, Xuan Liu, and Chang-Tien Lu. Spatial databases - accomplishments and research needs. *IEEE Trans. Knowl. and Data Eng.*, 11(1):45–55, 1999. DOI: 10.1109/69.755614 Cited on page(s) 9

Hyoseop Shin, Bongki Moon, and Sukho Lee. Adaptive multi-stage distance join processing. In *Proc. ACM SIGMOD Int. Conf. on Management of Data*, pages 343–354, 2000. DOI: 10.1145/335191.335428 Cited on page(s) 64

Yutao Shou, Nikos Mamoulis, Huiping Cao, Dimitris Papadias, and David W. Cheung. Evaluation of iceberg distance joins. In *Proc. 8th Int. Symp. Advances in Spatial and Temporal Databases*, pages 270–288, 2003. DOI: 10.1007/978-3-540-45072-6_16 Cited on page(s) 64

Yasin N. Silva, Xiaopeng Xiong, and Walid G. Aref. The RUM-tree: supporting frequent updates in r-trees using memos. *VLDB J.*, 18(3):719–738, 2009. DOI: 10.1007/s00778-008-0120-3 Cited on page(s) 117

A. Prasad Sistla, Ouri Wolfson, Sam Chamberlain, and Son Dao. Modeling and querying moving objects. In *Proc. 13th Int. Conf. on Data Engineering*, pages 422–432, 1997. DOI: 10.1109/ICDE.1997.581973 Cited on page(s) 116

Hans-Werner Six and Peter Widmayer. Spatial searching in geometric databases. In *Proc. 14th Int. Conf. on Data Engineering*, pages 496–503, 1988. DOI: 10.1109/ICDE.1988.105496 Cited on page(s) 32

Spiros Skiadopoulos, Christos Giannoukos, Panos Vassiliadis, Timos K. Sellis, and Manolis Koubarakis. Computing and handling cardinal direction information. In *Advances in Database*

Technology, Proc. 9th Int. Conf. on Extending Database Technology, pages 329–347, 2004. Cited on page(s) 18

Spiros Skiadopoulos, Nikos Sarkas, Timos K. Sellis, and Manolis Koubarakis. A family of directional relation models for extended objects. *IEEE Trans. Knowl. and Data Eng.*, 19(8):1116–1130, 2007. DOI: 10.1109/TKDE.2007.1046 Cited on page(s) 18

Michael Stonebraker, Paul Brown, and Dorothy Moore. *Object-Relational DBMSs*. Morgan Kaufmann, 1998. Cited on page(s) 9, 18

Chengyu Sun, Divyakant Agrawal, and Amr El Abbadi. Exploring spatial datasets with histograms. In *Proc. 18th Int. Conf. on Data Engineering*, pages 93–102, 2002a. Cited on page(s) 64

Chengyu Sun, Divyakant Agrawal, and Amr El Abbadi. Selectivity estimation for spatial joins with geometric selections. In *Advances in Database Technology, Proc. 8th Int. Conf. on Extending Database Technology*, 2002b. Cited on page(s) 64

Michael J. Swain and Dana H. Ballard. Color indexing. *Int J. Comput. Vision*, 7(1):11–32, 1991. DOI: 10.1007/BF00130487 Cited on page(s) 117

Latanya Sweeney. k-anonymity: A model for protecting privacy. *International Journal of Uncertainty, Fuzziness and Knowledge-Based Systems*, 10(5):557–570, 2002. Cited on page(s) 118

Pang-Ning Tan, Michael Steinbach, and Vipin Kumar. *Introduction to Data Mining*. Addison-Wesley, 2005. Cited on page(s) 118

Yufei Tao and Dimitris Papadias. MV3R-tree: A spatio-temporal access method for timestamp and interval queries. In *Proc. 27th Int. Conf. on Very Large Data Bases*, pages 431–440, 2001. Cited on page(s) 117

Yufei Tao and Dimitris Papadias. Time-parameterized queries in spatio-temporal databases. In *Proc. ACM SIGMOD Int. Conf. on Management of Data*, pages 334–345, 2002. Cited on page(s) 117

Yufei Tao, Dimitris Papadias, and Jimeng Sun. The TPR*-tree: An optimized spatio-temporal access method for predictive queries. In *Proc. 29th Int. Conf. on Very Large Data Bases*, pages 790–801, 2003. Cited on page(s) 117

Yufei Tao, Christos Faloutsos, Dimitris Papadias, and Bin Liu. Prediction and indexing of moving objects with unknown motion patterns. In *Proc. ACM SIGMOD Int. Conf. on Management of Data*, pages 611–622, 2004a. Cited on page(s) 117

Yufei Tao, Jun Zhang, Dimitris Papadias, and Nikos Mamoulis. An efficient cost model for optimization of nearest neighbor search in low and medium dimensional spaces. *IEEE Trans. Knowl. and Data Eng.*, 16(10):1169–1184, 2004b. Cited on page(s) 64

Yufei Tao, Vagelis Hristidis, Dimitris Papadias, and Yannis Papakonstantinou. Branch-and-bound processing of ranked queries. *Inf. Syst.*, 32(3):424–445, 2007. DOI: 10.1016/j.is.2005.12.001 Cited on page(s) 118

Yufei Tao, Cheng Sheng, and Jian Pei. On k-skip shortest paths. In *Proc. ACM SIGMOD Int. Conf. on Management of Data*, pages 421–432, 2011. Cited on page(s) 83

Paradise Team. Paradise: A database system for GIS applications. In *Proc. ACM SIGMOD Int. Conf. on Management of Data*, page 485, 1995. Cited on page(s) 9

Yannis Theodoridis and Timos K. Sellis. A model for the prediction of R-tree performance. In *Proc. 15th ACM SIGACT-SIGMOD-SIGART Symp. on Principles of Database Systems*, pages 161–171, 1996. Cited on page(s) 64

Yannis Theodoridis, Emmanuel Stefanakis, and Timos K. Sellis. Cost models for join queries in spatial databases. In *Proc. 14th Int. Conf. on Data Engineering*, pages 476–483, 1998. DOI: 10.1109/ICDE.1998.655810 Cited on page(s) 64

Roger Weber, Hans-Jörg Schek, and Stephen Blott. A quantitative analysis and performance study for similarity-search methods in high-dimensional spaces. In *Proc. 24th Int. Conf. on Very Large Data Bases*, pages 194–205, 1998. Cited on page(s) 117

Raymond Chi-Wing Wong and Ada Wai-Chee Fu. *Privacy-Preserving Data Publishing: An Overview*. Morgan & Claypool Publishers, 2010. Cited on page(s) 118

Michael F. Worboys and Matt Duckham. *GIS - a computing perspective (2nd ed.)*. Taylor & Francis, 2004. Cited on page(s) 9

Man Lung Yiu, Yufei Tao, and Nikos Mamoulis. The B^{dual}-tree: indexing moving objects by space filling curves in the dual space. *VLDB J.*, 17(3):379–400, 2008. DOI: 10.1007/s00778-006-0013-2 Cited on page(s) 117

Cui Yu, Beng Chin Ooi, Kian-Lee Tan, and H. V. Jagadish. Indexing the distance: An efficient method to kNN processing. In *Proc. 27th Int. Conf. on Very Large Data Bases*, pages 421–430, 2001. Cited on page(s) 117

Michael Zeiler. *Modeling our world: The ESRI Guide to Geodatabase Design*. ESRI Press, 1999. Cited on page(s) 9

Geraldo Zimbrao and Jano Moreira de Souza. A raster approximation for processing of spatial joins. In *Proc. 24th Int. Conf. on Very Large Data Bases*, pages 558–569, 1998. Cited on page(s) 64

Kai Zimmermann. Enhancing qualitative spatial reasoning - combining orientation and distance. In *Proc. Int. Conf. on Spatial Information Theory: A Theoretical Basis for GIS (COSIT)*, pages 69–76, 1993. Cited on page(s) 18

Author's Biography

NIKOS MAMOULIS

Nikos Mamoulis received a diploma in Computer Engineering and Informatics in 1995 from the University of Patras, Greece, and a PhD in Computer Science in 2000 from the Hong Kong University of Science and Technology. He is currently an associate professor at the Department of Computer Science, University of Hong Kong, which he joined in 2001. In the past, he has worked as a research and development engineer at the Computer Technology Institute, Patras, Greece and as a post-doctoral researcher at the Centrum voor Wiskunde en Informatica (CWI), the Netherlands. During 2008-2009 he was on leave to the Max-Planck Institute for Informatics (MPII), Germany. His research focuses on the management, mining, and privacy-preserving publishing of complex data, including spatial, spatio-temporal, object-relational, multimedia, text and semi-structured data. He has served on the program committees of over 80 international conferences and workshops on data management and data mining. He was the general chair of SSDBM 2008, the PC co-chair of SSTD 2009, and he participated in the organization committees of several other conferences and workshops. He is currently serving as an associate editor for IEEE TKDE and the VLBJ Journal. Besides, he is an editorial board member for Geoinformatica Journal and was a field editor of the Encyclopedia of Geographic Information Systems. He is a member of the ACM, IEEE, and the SSTD Endowment.

Printed in the United States
by Baker & Taylor Publisher Services